WEIRD YEARS
WITH JERRY STAHL

"I'm on a radiation vacation, soaking up the gammas."

Jerry Stahl writes dialogue that sings. His books, his screenplays, his writing all zing like little else. For pure beat poetry, look no further than the insanity in *Dr. Caligari*. The main problem with doing so has been, until the film's eventual rerelease on Blu-ray (coming soon from Mondo Macabro), even if you've *seen Dr. Caligari*, the available prints feature soundtracks so muddy that you can barely hear a thing, much less, *"I've got an EKG you can dance to. Everybody limbo!"*

If you're unfamiliar with *Dr. Caligari* or the "anti-porn" films Stahl made with Stephen Sayadian prior, *Nightdreams* and *Café Flesh* (under the pseudonym Herbert W. Day[1]), you might know his name from the Ben Stiller movie *Permanent Midnight*. It's based on Stahl's memoir of the same name, documenting his struggles as a working writer dealing with drug addiction.

"That was a thousand years ago, man," Stahl says to me when I bring up *Midnight*. "I've written at least nine books since then."

"Sure," I reply, "but I'm a really slow reader." I get a laugh.

"That was a very odd movie," he says. "I didn't write it, so I was a different kind of asshole in the movie than I was in the book. After we saw the screening, Ben and I went back and said that we were going to try and fix this. There were lines in that like, 'Jerry shoots up and gets the munchies,' which is really not how heroin works. I think he did an amazing job, all things considered. I was best man at his wedding, incidentally."

Some wild stories came out of Stahl's *Permanent Midnight* days. One tale came from *Twin Peaks* cocreator Mark Frost, who allegedly received a script from Stahl that

---

[1] "Well, the name I came up with, [Herbert W. Day], as you may know, was the name of a high school principal who used to swat me in front of the entire school, so it seemed like a good revenge to make him famous as a pornographer. Then, since we had 'Day,' maybe we should do something with 'Dream.' I don't know. It was probably just some drug-addled idea."

included a helicopter chase. "I think it had bloodstains on it," Frost says of the script. The prevailing theory is that Stahl confused *Twin Peaks* with another show he was working on at the time, possibly *Miami Vice*.

"Whatever," says Stahl. "It's probably true."

Stahl has a reputation for turning in "dark" scripts. He created the character of Lady Heather (played by Melinda Clarke, or "Mindy" to fans of *Return of the Living Dead III*) for *CSI*, a dominatrix that has an undisclosed relationship with William Petersen's character. If there was an episode of *CSI* dealing with "bizarre" fetishes, Stahl was the author.

"I was very lucky," Stahl says. "They paid me to be a weirdo. And it wasn't that I strived to work on TV. I got that gig because I used to go to the Hollywood YMCA, and one day, I bumped into Billy Petersen in the sauna, a rare nude encounter that actually resulted in work. I think he mentioned something like, 'Oh, yeah, my daughter read your book. I think I'm going to do this show in a couple of years; would you want to do it?' I said sure, and sure enough, man, he called me as soon as that show went on the air. That's how I got the gig. I got a chance to do a lot of wild shit on there, like infantilism, the furry stuff, crazy S and M shit…. I guess I created some sort of giant faux pas. I confused or conflated furries and plushies, and they really oppose each other, like Trotskyites and Stalinists. They marched in front of the CBS Building in New York in protest, saying I got it wrong. I guess I insulted them."

As for the "dark side" allegation, Stahl says: "I never knew it was a dark side. It was the only side I knew. Critics can give you labels, god bless them, but for my money, I never thought about being dark, or gallows humor; the life I'd led; or the childhood that got me there. That's just what I wrote. It's also the people I admired were the sort of black humorists. Terry Southern, Bruce Jay Friedman, Pynchon…again, those guys are my heroes, not that I can flatter myself for being near them, but that's the kind of stuff I'd always written. I've had some good years, yeah. Any time I tried to write 'normal,' it always came out completely grotesque. I had to find a way to have my voice. Even if I were writing some square show like *CSI*, I would find a way to make it bent. That was just the way I approached it."

Stahl became a writer the way most of us did: He found himself in situations worth writing about. "My family kind of fell apart," he says.

HAPPY CLOUD MEDIA, LLC, PRESENTS:

EXPLOITATION NATION

MR. BRUNELLE EXPLAINS IT ALL	2
DOWN THE RABBIT HOLE	3
THE *DR. CALIGARI* SECTION:	
DR. CALIGARI	6
WEIRD YEARS WITH JERRY STAHL	7
DANIEL BIRD: *DR. CALIGARI* RESTORATION	15
RINSE DREAM REVIVAL WITH STEPHEN SAYADIAN	21
FROM *HI-FEAR* TO *HI-8* WITH BRAD SYKES	25
NO MORE WAITING, HERE'S CHARLES PINION	31
NO REGRETS, BY TIM RITTER	37
REVIEWS	47
NON-OBJECTIVE REVIEWS	50
SATURN'S CORE	53
OH, FFS, ANOTHER AD?	58
INDONESIAN HORROR	59
A DIGRESSION ABOUT TRANSGRESSION	64
CINEMA OF TRANSGRESSION MANIFESTO	65
TRUST THE WITCH: LYDIA LUNCH AND RETROVIRUS	67
I'D BUY THAT FOR A DOLLAR!	71
"THE MOVIES AREN'T NUMBERS," SAYS JUSTIN SEAMAN	77
FORCE OF ZANE HERSHBERGER	83

Exploitation Nation
is published by
Happy Cloud Media, LLC
Vol. 1, No. 13 © 2022

Amy Lynn Best:
Publisher
Mike Watt:
Editor-in-Chief
Ally Melling:
Editor
Carolyn Haushalter:
Asst. Editor
Gianna Leonne:
Transcription

Contributors:
**Dr. Rhonda Baughman
Robert Waldo Brunelle, Jr.
Mike Haushalter
Jason Lane
Tim Ritter
J.M. Channell**

Cover and Art Direction by:
Ryan Hose

Special thanks to:
**Brad Sykes, Charles Pinion,
Daniel Bird, Ross Snyder,
William Hellfire, Jerry Stahl,
and Steven Sayadian**

All photographic and artistic content is copyright of the original holders and is included here for promotional purposes only. No rights are implicit or implied.

Exploitation Nation is published periodically by Happy Cloud Media, LLC, (Amy Lynn Best and Mike Watt, P.O. Box 816, Venetia, PA 15367). **Exploitation Nation** Issue #13 (ISBN 978-1-951036-29-4) is © 2022 by Happy Cloud Media, LLC. All rights reserved. All featured articles and illustrations are copyright © 2022 by their respective writers and artists. Reproductions of any material in whole or in part without its creator's written permission are strictly forbidden. **Exploitation Nation** accepts no responsibility for unsolicited manuscripts, DVDs, stills, art, or any other materials. Contributions are accepted on an invitational basis only.
Visit us at: www.exploitation-nation.com, Facebook.com/ExploitationNation, and www.happycloudpublishing.com.

DOWN THE RABBIT HOLE

Linear time, man. It gets us all.

There's this outfit called Saturn's Core—a division of Vinegar Syndrome—run by journalist and promoter Ross Snyder and filmmaker Bill Hellfire, and they've been doing the Lord's work lately (whoever she might be), restoring and rereleasing some classic movies from the by-gone shot-on-video (SOV) era. Saturn's Core is playing around in the early '90s at the moment, introducing new audiences to things like Eric Stanze's *Savage Harvest* and our own Scooter McCrae's *Shatter Dead*. And lemme tell ya, it's fucking surreal.

Amy Lynn Best and I formed Happy Cloud Pictures in 1998, and we joined the indie filmmaking scene with our short film *Tenants*. Filmmaker Ron Bonk (*The Vicious Sweet*) had a distribution company called Salt City Video, and he picked up *Tenants* for an anthology film called *Cutting Edge: The Night Basement*, hosted by Michael Legge (*Braindrainer*) and including another short by Michael Gingold, then associate editor of *Fangoria*. Ron included *Tenants* in the lineup for the 1998 B-Movie Film Festival in Syracuse, New York, and that's where we met so many other indie filmmakers suffering the same struggles, frustrations, and youthful ambitions we were.

Ross considers the mid-'90s the "second wave" of indie SOV filmmaking. (The late Andy Copp [*The Mutilation Man*] and I set it around the year 2000, but that's neither here nor there.) The fact is we were following in the footsteps of J.R. Bookwalter and *The Dead Next Door*, Tim Ritter and *Truth or Dare?*, Jim VanBebber and *Deadbeat at Dawn*, Mike Lackey and the *Street Trash* crew, and even Frank Henenlotter, who'd paved the way for all of us with *Basket Case*. These were all folks who'd proven you didn't need a bazillion dollars to make an entertaining movie. The SOV guys were just making do with S-VHS and Hi-8mm tape.

The indie horror industry was, and I don't say this lightly, fucking insane. No one was making bank, but many of us were earning enough to make the next movie. Everything was on a shoestring budget, with the majority of the money going toward tape stock and Karo syrup. The goal was to get into Blockbuster, but the formula was violent gore plus nudity, two things Blockbuster hated but audiences couldn't get enough of. The edict was clear: As long as you had tits and gore,

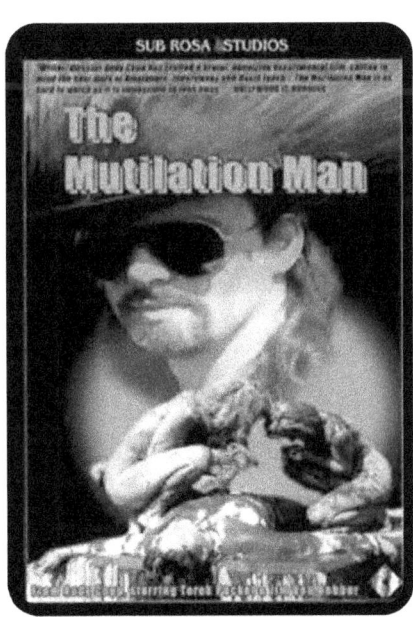

you could get away with telling any kind of story.

And the SOV indies *did*. For those who grew up in the '90s, every news story led with the prophecy of doom: Generation X would never succeed the way our Boomer parents did. The economy was against us, and yet, somehow, that was our fault. Even before we could vote, we were told in no uncertain terms that slinging French fries was the best for which an entire generation could hope. We crawled out from beneath the shadow of a near-constant threat of nuclear war, thanks to the asshole oligarchs running the Cold War (Gee, the more things change…); unemployment was through the roof; and mom-and-pop video stores were the only escape.

We were an angry, frustrated group of young people heading toward the millennium, and even *then*, we were told that on the stroke of midnight, the entire world could shut down because no one was smart enough to teach the computers running our world that the number after 1999 wasn't 0000. We were all convinced we'd be living *Mad Max*-style come January 1, 2000. When that didn't happen, we returned to making the most misanthropic, cynical, violent, sinister movies we could imagine.

A quick look at Saturn's Core's initial offerings includes: Stanze's *Savage Harvest*, McCrae's *Shatter Dead*, a Charles Pinion double feature consisting of *We Await* and *Red Spirit Lake*, and Ronnie Sortor's *Sinistre*. They're all studies in violence and misanthropy. *Red Spirit Lake* and *Savage Harvest* offer traditional protagonists caught in otherworldly situations beyond their control. Contrast these with the other films, which feature only antiheroes. In *Shatter Dead*, Susan (Stark Raven) is merely attempting to make her way home to her boyfriend, beset on all sides by undead (or, more specifically, *still dead*) people, now a section of third-class citizens to whom she is cold and even murderous. In *Sinistre*, vicious criminals encounter an evil worse than themselves. There is no such thing as a happy ending in these types of films, and the filmmakers would be offended by the suggestion.

As Gen X artists felt besieged and ignored by the mainstream, so too did our characters. Only punk outfits like *Film Threat*, *Alt Cinema*, and *Fango* appreciated what we were doing: primal screams with some inventive photography, pushing the boundaries of violence, sex, and bad taste. Often, there's a gleeful sadism to these narratives. As artists, we hope you, the audience, fucking suffer as much as the characters. The world is a harsh, horrific place, one filled with things we can't understand, not from other humans, not from things otherwise.

For so long, the formula worked. Even as Netflix stomped over the few remaining mom-and-pop video stores that had survived the Blockbuster juggernaut, indie film propped up the industry. Sometime around 2010, Netflix decided it didn't need us anymore, and it decreased its indie collection almost overnight. In 2015, Amazon Prime did the same.

We used to joke that Hollywood was trying to destroy us. They didn't want the competition. This was defensive joking. We were all terrified that, ultimately, our punk rock explosions of horror just weren't up to snuff, and that the mainstream we professed to hate didn't want us anyway. The "truth" was that Hollywood was blissfully unaware of our existence. Until it wasn't. Suddenly, indies were a threat to that precious streaming revenue. Even as Hollywood continually decreased the amount our hard-fought productions *earned* on its sites, it continued to marginalize us. Finally, it purged itself of our stain.

It's both gratifying and terrifying the way the old is being embraced now. Saturn's Core, Vinegar Syndrome, Severin—they're bringing back titles that would have otherwise been lost to the ether. At the same time, indie filmmakers are finding it more and more difficult to raise money for *new* productions. While preserving our catalogs for Gen Z (for my money, the potential saviors of the world) is great, investors are shy to fund something new. And who can blame them? There are fewer independent distributors now than ever. If our movies can't be seen, why make them?

Plus, let's face it: Most of us are *tired*, man. If we aren't past our 50s, we're careening toward them. Sure, the iPhone 13 shoots in 4K, which is better than any camera we had in the 2000s. It fits in your pocket, and you can take it anywhere. But what about lighting? Sound? Sure, the pandemic taught us that we can survive with minimal outside contact, and sure, pandemic-based movies are all over Tubi…actually, I don't know what point I was trying to make here. See? Tired.

So, this issue of *ExNat* spotlights "what was old is new again." For all our sakes (and our survival), I hope this current trend sticks around for a while. We all have backstock we'd like to unload.

Stephen Sayadian (aka Rinse Dream)'s *Dr. Caligari* (1989) is finally coming to Blu-ray. I know you already know this because I won't shut up about it on social media. If you're not excited about it, it's because you haven't seen it already.

To celebrate Mondo Macabro's titanic work of restoration, we're here with three brand-new interviews with those behind the mind-melting masterpiece: author Jerry Stahl, restorationist Daniel Bird, and director Sayadian.

It was Bird's respect and love for the film that got the restoration going. As he tells *ExNat* in his piece, "...*Dr. Caligari* is completely *sui generis*—the only place it truly comes from is Stephen Sayadian. This is someone who developed a style that was pop, explicit, anarchistic, surrealistic, and then fine-tuned it through one-sheets, box art, album covers, and not just film, but also theatre and music videos. The result is *Dr. Caligari*."

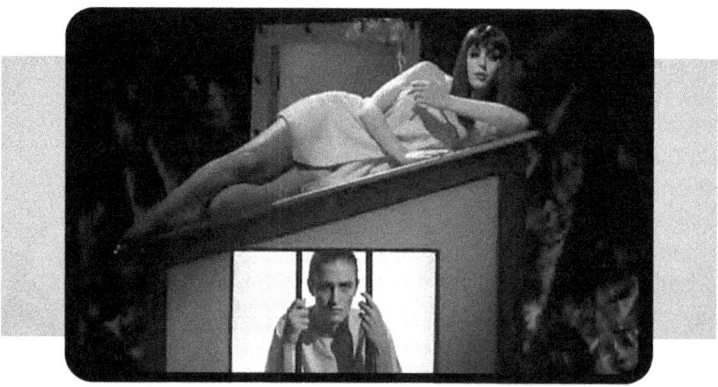

Laura Albert as Mrs. Van Houten (top) assumes control over Dr. Caligari (Madeleine Reynal, below). Confused? You won't be after Mondo Macabro's release of *Dr. Caligari*! (Photo courtesy Stephen Sayadian. All Rights Reserved.)

"My old man checked himself out. It got weird, and I got shipped away. I went to Europe and wandered around. A lot of people do that. I knocked around a bit, sure. I had the great ability to be uncomfortable anywhere. That's probably helped me out. The only thing that's harder than writing is not writing. I've always had a hard time, like a lot of people in life, with not fitting in, not possessing that rule book you feel everyone else was born with. So, when you lose yourself in writing, you forget about all of it. All those nightmares become, like Iggy Pop says, 'some weird gift.' I've been lucky, because without it, what do you do [as a writer]? If you're an accountant and you have all that weird shit and experience and shame, whatever the fuck, what are you going to do? As a writer, you can turn it into something, and if you're lucky, a couple of people [get it]. I'm kind of a cult guy, I guess. There are people who really relate to it, but I'm not John Grisham, you know? It's like Hemingway said: 'Travel broadens the ass.'"

As an aside, this leads us into a Hemingway conversation. As it turns out, neither of us is a fan, but only one of us wrote *Hemingway and Gellhorn*. "I'm *not* a Hemingway fan," Stahl says, "but I really admired Martha Gellhorn. I thought she was a fearless woman and a great writer. I kind of jammed her into the title to justify her. Hemingway, I mean, God bless him, he's not my cup of tea, but I know a lot of people love him. Listen, people gotta worship who they worship. He's an American God, you know. I do like the fact that his mother made him wear dresses as a boy. Gotta love that.

Stahl himself (Photo courtesy Jerry Stahl.)

He got electroshock, and it destroyed his memory. He was supposed to write a speech for JFK's inauguration, and with no memory, he just couldn't write. His first suicide attempt, he tried to walk into a plane propeller at an airport. I love the guy for that. I respect anyone who suffers the way he suffered. And he really did. And, come on, it's not like he was the first writer who was a dick. Jesus, show me a writer who *isn't* a dick."

"Present company excepted," I say.

"No, no, I'm as dickish as the next guy."

"I was talking about me." We laugh.

Knocking around led Stahl to Columbus, Ohio, where he booked a gig with Larry Flynt's *Hustler* magazine. He was hired and fired by Paul Krassner. "I have nothing against Krassner," Stahl says. "The guy was a legend. *The Realist* was an amazing fucking magazine. I was just going through some shit at the time and was probably a bit of a douchebag. I have no beef with him. I mean, he fired me, but he had every right to fire me. I was just a young idiot then. I didn't realize the reverence he was due, and that's on me."

But it was at *Hustler* that Stahl met Sayadian. Sayadian was the magazine's art director, putting together hilarious and profane ads for products. "We met in Columbus [at *Hustler*]," Stahl explains. "He would come up with these scenarios and say, 'We need dialogue here.' I would just bang it out. Generally, if he would laugh or react, I knew I'd, you know…we just had a vein that we mined, no pun intended. A couple of drug-addled young maniacs being as creative as we could in a way that nobody really seemed to have done."

Talk to anyone who has worked closely with Sayadian and a pattern emerges: Love and respect run deep with this crew. Sayadian is clear in his interviews and has said in these very pages that his favorite method of collaborating with Stahl is when "I would write ten pages, give them to Jerry, and then, he'd change the entire thing, always for the better."

But even before I mention this, Stahl insists: "Make sure and say that I think Steve is the Jean Cocteau of his generation, one of the great unsung American geniuses, whose time—against all odds—is finally here."

Though Sayadian's visual style is unique, he gives his collaborators abject freedom. Stahl elaborates, saying, "I do know that when working with Stephen—and I've worked with other directors who do this, but particularly with Steve—he'll say, 'Here are the dots you have to connect.' I didn't have to stress about plot or anything like that. I could just wail. We have a very kindred sensibility, some weird hybrid of, you know, Pynchon meets men's mags of the '50s, meets pulp, meets demented opiated, bizarro spew that somehow works with these characters. I don't think anyone else would want that kind of dialogue. But lucky for me, it worked for Steve.

"I was just very lucky to meet up with Steve. Our connection's deep. We go back very far, and when you have somebody who gets you, it's priceless. It's the best thing in the world. My introduction to [*Caligari*] publically was that I wanted to impress a date somewhere back in the godforsaken '90s. I took her to a multiplex for a midnight screening, for which, impressively, we were the only people in the audience. To have this come back as some kind of popular French- and Euro-appreciated avant-garde classic is beyond unexpected and very gratifying."

"Stephen told me your words are the nerves and blood of his films," I say.

"I've been called worse!" Stahl replies. "I love the guy. We're like brothers. We didn't talk for, Jesus, decades, and then, out of the blue, he calls and asks me to do [this new script, *Hell Is Tender*]. There's a great Henry Miller definition of friendship: 'A friend is someone who you don't see for ten years, and when you do, you can't stop talking.' It's just nice, again, when people get you. And Steve's one of those people who, when you're talking with him, you feel smarter when you're done. He uses these incredibly odd, bizarro, interesting, arcane references and knows more about film than *anybody* I've ever talked to, including *New York Times* film critics I've known. He's just an amazing, encyclopedic font of twisted cinema history. Lucky for me, our paths crossed. It's not like anyone else is begging me to write that kind of dialogue, let's just face it. I've never really fit in in Hollywood. I've made a career of it over the years—some weird years—but it's not like working with Steve, where it's just go, go, go, man—just as out there as you want to be."

Stahl and Sayadian's first film collaboration was the post-apocalyptic *Nightdreams*, a pornographic forerunner of *Dr. Caligari*. In the film, sexual paralytic Mrs. Van Houten is haunted by erotic nightmares...involving sentient and well-hung Cream of Wheat boxes and adult babies gnawing on bones. The beat poetry there rivals the surreal imagery.

Following that, the pair did *Café Flesh*. The film is set after the bombs have been dropped and society has been divided into two groups. One of the groups, the Sex Positives, put on shows for the majority, the Sex Negatives. *Café Flesh* is a cabaret of cruelty that features an early performance from Scream Queen Michelle Bauer (billed as Pia Snow).

After the deliberate sex show that was *Nightdreams*, the principals made a decision while making *Café Flesh*.

"We wanted the most *non*-arousing sex in the world [in *Café Flesh*]," says Stahl. "I'm sure Steve has told you the story about watching a bunch of Japanese tourists fleeing the Pussycat Theatre on Santa Monica Boulevard in droves out of just sheer horror and revulsion. So, we knew we were doing something right."

Making *Café Flesh* is an adventure that deserves its own film. "Sure, we were trying to get something going on film," Stahl says, "and the only way we could get it was to make this movie where, as you know, the guys would pay us in quarters from the peep show. We had to sneak through the Cave Theatre, which had stalactites and stalagmites up and down the ceiling and the floor. These poor guys in raincoats were yelling at us, 'Get down! Move!' as we were going up to the office. An enormously fat man would hand us a bag of quarters, saying, 'Go.' He said, 'You know, boys, we like what you're doing. We just need eight more scenes.' And then we had to come up with the 'money scenes.' Just because we were punks and idiots, we came up with the non-arousing sex scenes. I've heard people say they never wanted to have sex again after that movie."

Dr. Caligari was an effort to remake *Nightdreams* without the penetration. The basic story was retained: Mrs. Van Houten is forced to stay at a sexual mental facility, where her fantasies are used against her, but with the added level that the titular character is the granddaughter of the famous German Expressionist psychophysician. The result is a hilarious, neon-colored grotesquerie that dances with softcore but splashes around in the viewer's own limbic fluid.

"Elaborate, please."

"Blankety-blank-blank."
"Thanks for elaborating."

"Pornography used to be subversive," I comment.

"Not anymore," Stahl agrees. "I think pornography is the squarest fucking thing in the world, especially now! S and M is about as arousing as a Bloomingdale's catalog. It's very square, very accepted, and pretty vanilla right now. So, I don't think there's anything subversive about porn. Far from it. Sure, at the time we were making it, it was still a nasty, dark corner of the planet. But not now."

Although Stahl and Sayadian were working at one of the raunchiest magazines on the stands at the time, porn wasn't on either of their minds. "I was just trying to be a writer, man," says Stahl. "I think by then, I'd written four or five unpublished novels. I'd

Stahl and Lydia Lunch (Photo by Oliver Maxwell Kupper. All Rights Reserved.)

publish short stories here and there. I'd done a lot of journalism before. *Hustler* was just a gig. I didn't give a shit about *Hustler*; I didn't even read it. When I met Steve, I thought he was cool, but I didn't think in terms of *Hustler*. It was great. Larry Flynt did some funny shit, but that wasn't where I was at.

"I was just trying to survive off my prose. It never even occurred to me to write movies. I never thought about writing movies. To this day, I don't know how to write movies. But Steve just said, 'Fill in the blanks,' and we had such a great time doing it. The great thing about collaboration is you got a reason to hang with someone you love hanging with. That's really what it was all about. It's great to be appreciated, man. It's great when someone gets you, especially after you've faced a ton of rejection, as I have (and did at the time)."

For all the drama in *Permanent Midnight*, there's nothing bitter or even angry in Stahl's voice. He's more intent on celebrating Sayadian's newfound success outside the cult cinema world: "I'm so happy for Steve, you know? More than anything, I'm glad that he's getting appreciated in his own lifetime. If I'm part of that, fantastic. But that's the big part for me, that he's vindicated."

Of course, it's not like Stahl has been whiling away his time in stasis. "I can't afford to take a break," he says. "I worked with my old friend Stiller on the limited series *Escape at Dannemora*, which Ben directed for Showtime, and which got me an Emmy nomination. But basically, I just work on books. The Hollywood shit, I do with my left hand. If it works out, great. It's always iffy. So, I'm starting another novel, even as we speak.

"I also have a book coming out next summer that I just finished, *Nein, Nein, Nein!*, which is based on a six-part series I did for VICE. It's about taking a bus tour of concentration camps with tourists from the Midwest who had never seen a Jew. It was a completely uncomfortable bit of journalism while my own life was falling apart. It's about the Holocaust, it's about taking a bus tour with a bunch of strangers, and it's about being hired to write a pilot about my wonderful fun life as an older dad with a young kid after my marriage had already fallen apart. The kid was living in a different state, which was just a bizarre situation. It's about failure—blowing a bunch of gigs in Hollywood—while wondering what people who went to concentration camps thought about. Did their huge problems become petty? It's about all of that stuff. It's kind of a dangerous book because it's a funny book, but it's also about what it's about. That's the most recent thing that…I think I'm proud of. It's on VICE.com. They called it 'A Tour of Hell, from Hell.'"

I pause then for a moment, trying to wrap my head around the idea of concentration camp bus tours, because I'm often sickeningly naïve when it comes to the horrors of the world.

"Somehow, just sitting there, looking at the…you can't visit the Auschwitz Snack Bar without changing a little bit," Stahl says. "What's supposed to go through your head watching people chow down on pizza fifteen feet from the crematorium? I went through a lot of stuff, as one does. Steve was very helpful with the book as I was writing it. I'd send it to him, and he's a good gauge of false and real and what doesn't work/what works. If he's laughing, I know I'm doing something right. And see, I don't consider it 'dark.' To me, it's just reality. Another person can put that label on it, which is fine. We live in dark times. Read the fucking paper, read the *New York Times*. Is it dark?"

"Maybe," I say, "but it's rarely funny."

"Fair," Stahl replies. "I'm not making, you know, *joke*-jokes. You're putting yourself in these odd situations, which is always the kind of journalism I did. I always loved gonzo, where part of it is about what it's about, but it's also about your reaction to what the fuck is going on. I used to write about, you know, 'Nude Singles Weekends in Topanga,' which was incredibly uncomfortable. But from the discomfort, you get some kind of jam, if you're lucky."

"I know you're Jewish, but that sounds really Catholic."

"Is there a difference anymore?" he asks, and we laugh. "I don't even know. As my grandfather used to say, 'If you forget you're a Jew, a Gentile will remind you.'"

Lenny Bruce said the same thing.

As our conversation draws to a close, we start shooting the shit about Pittsburgh (Stahl lived in a neighborhood not too far from my stomping grounds), and I ask if he has anything else he wants to add.

"Just in terms of *Caligari*; I just want to say that I'm so gratified," Stahl says. "I mean, Steve called me yesterday and said the fucking Pompidou Centre is going to do a screening in Paris, which is just hilarious, beyond anything I ever expected! I don't know much about life, but I know that weird shit happens if you don't die young. This is living proof yet again. Who knows? After all is said and done, maybe it'll be *Dr. Caligari* as our legacy."

And what a legacy, to be appreciated by so few but admired by so many.

"We should all be so lucky," Stahl adds.

Nein, Nein, Nein!: One Man's Tale of Depression, Psychic Torment, and a Bus Tour of the Holocaust is slated to be released on July 5, 2022.

DANIEL BIRD: DR. CALIGARI RESTORATION

Martin Scorsese's Film Foundation claims that "half of all American films made before 1950 and over 90 percent of films made before 1929 are lost forever."[1] Silent films were printed on stock that used silver nitrate as a backing. Most of those movies were melted down during WWII to reclaim the silver. Full collections of films have been found warped and turned to vinegar, stored in damp basements for decades at a time.

Many moons ago, I worked in the Optical Department at WRS Motion Picture and Video Lab, using terrible equipment to restore films photochemically. We had a frame scanner, but nobody knew how it worked. Three decades later and restoration is all the rage again, with computers battling the ravages of linear time.

Daniel Bird is, in many ways, the poster child for ExNat. It's meant as a compliment.

"Truly honored to be a poster child for *Exploitation Nation*," he writes, accepting the compliment on its face.

By saying Bird is the poster child, I mean he has a foot in both the world of "agreed classic film" and the much-derided "exploitation" end of things. Like us, he doesn't delineate between high and low art. It's all of a piece, and it all deserves to be preserved. Art is art is art.

Bird spearheaded the efforts to restore the films of Rinse Dream (aka our friend Stephen Sayadian),

"He speaks for the films so they will not be forgotten." (Photo courtesy Daniel Bird.)

---

1 Mikesell, Terry. "Group's Rescue of Old Films Preserves Glimpse into Past." *The Film Foundation*, Directors Guild of America, www.film-foundation.org/columbus-dispatch.

particularly the much-anticipated Blu-ray of *Dr. Caligari*. And here's where we begin.

When I worked at WRS film lab, one of the little platitudes in the telecine room read, "Restorationists live in the past to inform the present." (Since it was a crummy place to work, the plaque was the object of cynical scorn, of course.) Do you agree with this?

Almost. Let me answer by separating two related but distinct impulses: The first is to study filmmaking, the second is to practice filmmaking. You can't, in my opinion, practice filmmaking without studying it. Of course, mastering certain technical things is one thing; developing a style or a command of form is something else. On the one hand, I do think an awareness of the past is important, but I also recognize it as a burden. I often get the feeling that filmmakers who came to prominence during the '90s (Tarantino, PTA, etc.) often get trapped in a hall of mirrors, but that's postmodernism for you. Ignorance of the past is just that: ignorance. Empty vessels make the most noise, etc. I think all technical and formal advancements involve a step back to go forward, so to speak. The best example is *2001: A Space Odyssey*. Technically, it was cutting edge for its time, but the concepts (e.g., rewinding the film and running the same strip through the camera) are as old as cinema itself.

I'd say something similar about Parajanov's *The Color of Pomegranates* too. I have this theory that 1968 is the year when what should have happened in 1928 (when sound was introduced) finally happened. Instead, the very thing that Eisenstein warned against happened: We used sound to film stage plays. I have a simple test that most films don't pass: If I can close my eyes and still follow the plot, what I am watching is not cinema, but rather a filmed radio play. I'm interested in the relationship between sight and sound. The only thing I don't agree with in the platitude is that I don't feel like I'm living in the past. What is more, the business of looking to the past is not to inform the present, but rather the future. Again, *2001* is a good example.

For the uninitiated, how do you define "restoration"? What work went into bringing Dr. Caligari *to Blu-ray for the first time?*

As the word suggests, to restore a film means to return it to its former condition. *Dr. Caligari* is a great example. It was shot on 35mm negative and printed and projected on 35mm in the standard ratio, 1.85:1. Now, when it was released on video, one of these prints was telecined (i.e., turned to video, in standard definition); this simply reflects the available technology back then. As the TV standard was 4:3 back then, the frame was composed that way too. TV screens were smaller back then, and only the film freaks liked letterboxing. Despite getting great reviews, *Dr. Caligari* really only found its audience on laser disc and video. So, for the last three decades, this is how people have seen *Dr. Caligari*: in the wrong ratio, in standard definition. What is more, all those theatrical prints seem to have disappeared too. So, what we've done is track down the original camera negative (the film that went through the camera), clean it, scan it, and then digitally get rid of all those imperfections that are the result of previous handling and 30 years of storage.

In the case of *Dr. Caligari*, the negative wasn't kept in laboratory conditions. So, the result is that what you are seeing [on the Blu-ray], for the first time since [the film's] projection in cinemas, is *Dr. Caligari* how it was meant to be seen. It's a little better in fact, because the negative obviously has more resolution than the release prints. Also, we've gone back to the original magnetic sound reels and transferred those to digital. There was a mixing error in the opening titles, so we've been able to sort that out at the request of Stephen and [composer Mitchell Froom].

However, as for me, I'm not a technician, and restoration simply means reestablishing *Dr. Caligari*'s place as arguably the last midnight movie. Honestly, I still don't quite understand how the film could open with such great reviews and then practically disappear, but it did. So, thanks to Mondo Macabro, it's finally getting the release it deserves.

For the non-film addict, the idea of restoring an odd, erotic, art-house comedy would seem like a funny waste of time. Fortunately, we don't have non-film addicts reading us. Still, why did you personally feel Dr. Caligari *deserved restoration? Can you talk about your love for the film?*

It certainly wasn't a waste of time for me, as *Dr. Caligari* was in genuine danger. There are no release prints in any collections I know of, and the negative and sound were not stored

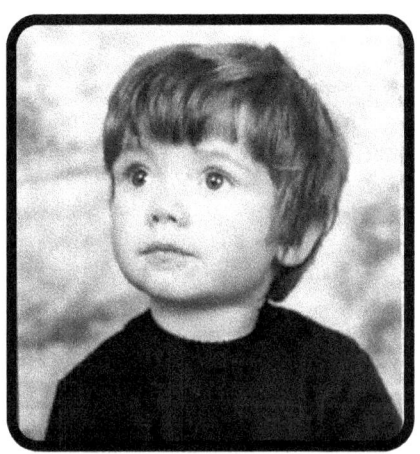

"Funny Caption Coming."
(Photo courtesy Daniel Bird.)

in a laboratory, so despite having a cult reputation, it could so easily have been lost and only exist on the internet as a murky, full-frame, standard-definition video master. It *is* important because, in many ways, *Dr. Caligari* is the culmination of Sayadian's work up until that point in his career. For me personally, *Dr. Caligari* is completely *sui generis*—the only place it truly comes from is Stephen Sayadian. This is someone who developed a style that was pop, explicit, anarchistic, surrealistic, and then fine-tuned it through one-sheets, box art, album covers, and not just film, but also theatre and music videos. The end result is *Dr. Caligari*. It's got all the pop culture references years before Tarantino. At the same time, Stahl's wordplay is more surrealistic—Prévert for perverts, if you will. It looks as good as a Powell and Pressburger film when they were working with Hein Heckroth. I honestly think Sayadian is a fellow traveler of Lynch—someone who began with one foot in the visual arts and the other in the midnight circuit. Their worlds are related but very different. Lynch, for me, is more thick, dense, heavy, woozy. Sayadian is light, sharp, electric, piercing. Sayadian, in his own way, is as influential as Lynch, but not directly; rather, by proxy. A lot of people riffed on his style, not just in film, but also the *Hustler* layouts, album covers and theatre work, especially *Jackie Charge*[2]. It is not just a style, it's a sensibility.

There's already buzz about the upcoming Blu-ray, but what features are you particularly proud to have gotten onto the disc (beyond beautifying one of the most stunning indie movies ever made)?

Well, the full specs haven't been announced, but I can say that we filmed a long interview with Stephen and recorded an audio commentary. As you can imagine, he took great care in the look of the frame, not to mention the backdrop. So, in a way, it's not just an extra, but rather a film in itself. Also, the commentary is not just him talking over a film; he really goes into specifics. The only problem is that *Caligari* is just 80 minutes long!

---

2 *Jackie Charge* is a play Jerry Stahl wrote in the 1980s, starring Fox Harris as a Peeping Tom who "becomes a kind of hero," as Stahl tells Lydia Lunch in an article written for Tin House (https://tinhouse.com/difficult-happiness-a-conversation-between-jerry-stahl-and-lydia-lunch/). "It was supposed to run for two weeks but ended up doing six months at the Gene Dynarski Theater on Sunset Boulevard. Timothy Leary came a couple of times. It became kind of a Thing." *Jackie Charge* grew out of a screenplay that Stahl and Sayadian were writing. "After [*Café Flesh*], there were all kinds of offers for movies, and for no reason that I can remember, we didn't pursue any of them and did a play instead."

I spent a good deal of my professional career chasing Stephen down only to "meet" him by chance, and I found him to be every bit the charming iconoclast I'd hoped he'd be. How is Stephen to work with, and how was the Dr. Caligari *process to do together?*

I have learned a lot from working with Stephen. He oozes talent (and knows it), but he doesn't feel the need to prove it. As you know, he had a medical crisis that put his career on hiatus. A lesser person would be bitter and resentful at the lost opportunities. Not Stephen. On the contrary, he comes across as content and someone who feels very fortunate. I have just read the latest draft of his new script with Stahl, *Hell Is Tender*. On the one hand, it is, I would say, the third part of a suite made up of *Café Flesh* and *Dr. Caligari*. On the other hand, it has two things those films don't: a real plot and a heart. Admittedly, it is a heart wrapped in barbed wire, hanging in black space, surrounded by smoke—but a heart nonetheless. This very much reflects where Stephen is at now. My fingers, toes, and everything else I have two sets of are crossed in the hope that these images and words jump from page to screen.

You worked hard to bring Walerian Borowczyk back to the public's (cineaste's) attention. Every Borowczyk fan has a different take on the man's work. What is yours?

Borowczyk's predicament was, in its own way, very similar to Sayadian's: You look at the work and think, *Why isn't this stuff everywhere?* Of course, it is the same thing: a certain narrow-mindedness on the part of some critics, coupled with somewhat banal things, like rights, storage, and distribution. Borowczyk is the filmmaker I always go back to. I get a lot of pleasure from watching his films, particularly the shorts, *Renaissance*, *Les jeux des anges*, *Le dictionnaire de Joachim*, *Rosalie*, *Gavotte*, and *Diptyque*. In many ways, I think you could say his innovation mirrored Sayadian's: They both developed highly original work in print and then made it move. They both work in this dark, surrealistic area that touches on sex and horror. They're both humorists. What's not to like?

You also produced two documentaries based on films dear to me, Possession *and* Knife in the Water, *both difficult films, both important to film history. I'm not sure there's a question here beyond this: What draws you to these types of complicated films?*

In the case of *Knife in the Water*, I had just moved to Warsaw. I had been awarded a post-graduate scholarship to study in Poland. This was from the Polish Ministry of Education. They probably regret that decision now. I had published a short book on Polanski, and I was contacted by the people making documentaries not just about *Knife in the Water*, but also about *Repulsion* and *Cul-de-sac*. So, basically, my job was as a researcher and location-fixer. I suggested whom to interview, found how to contact them, set up the interviews, and prepared the questions. In a few cases, I conducted the interviews myself. So, it was a dream come true, meeting all these dinosaurs who are all now gone—Wajda, Morgenstern, Malanowicz, Gutowski, Niemczyk, etc.

In the case of *Possession*, I simply thought that the film needed some context. The German distributors were preparing to release the film for the first time in Germany, on the twentieth anniversary of the fall of the Berlin Wall, so they thought it necessary too. I feel very lucky to have known and, in some cases, worked with such people as Borowczyk, Żuławski, and Sayadian. It's been a privilege to work on projects relating to both Aleksei German and Parajanov. I never thought I'd be working with Criterion on releases of *Come and See* and *The Ascent*. To answer your question, what draws me to these films and filmmakers is that they all have something in common: a look.

Are there films you would personally love to see restored for current generations? Anything you feel has fallen through the cracks over the years? (Jeez, there's a loaded question.)

Nightdreams. It appears that

only two incomplete prints survive. I challenged Sayadian to remake it exactly. *Nightdreams Recurring*. Again, is this about the past or the present?

Both the undereducated and the effete might ask, "Why bother restoring 'those kinds' of films?" I feel both groups harm serious discourse about film. Is there anything you would say to the snobs at both ends of the spectrum (from the "I just wanna be entertained" end to the "If it doesn't have Tibetan throat singers in it, it's too commercial" end)?

There's nothing wrong with undereducation if you're open to education, as we all should be. Conversely, there is a problem if you consider that you know all that there is to know. I don't consider the past either known or concrete. It is constantly changing. Look through history and every major book is either a riposte or a response to something else. It's a dialogue, sometimes (but not always) with the dead. Beckett started off copying Joyce, but he realized it was a dead end, and the way forward, for him, was to react against Joyce. It's the ultimate compliment. Give me Bresson or Żuławski; I honestly don't care. One purged the frame and soundtrack, the other overstuffed it. Neither was right or wrong; both offered essential dialogues with Dostoevsky. I wish, as I am sure Paul Schrader does, Bresson made a porn film. On the one hand, that sounds the height of bad taste. On the other, it recognizes that there is a sweet spot between the listless numbness of an overfucked porn player and one of Bresson's models, who are about as human as the isotypes plastered to toilet doors—and I believe that was exactly Bresson's point: a sort of cinema language.

There's no such thing as a guilty pleasure to those who love film, but there are titles we hesitate to bring up among our peers. For instance, when I defend Grease 2 *to the* Film Threat *crowd, the bike chains come out. Is there anything you love, but with caution?*

I experience guilt, but not about cinema. I have guiltlessly talked my way out of an appreciation of crash-zooms into Lina Romay's crotch, probably with reference to Michael Snow or something insufferably pretentious like that. If I ever felt guilty pleasure about a film, it would be for something like *Hunger*, by Steve McQueen, not Andy Milligan. It's not an ideology but a reflex action. The saying "Treat a princess like a whore and a whore like a princess," well, the "princesses" of cinema (and I say that in a modern, gender-neutral way—I'm just mixing my metaphors, as usual) are often the real "whores" of cinema. Both McQueen and Ken Loach made commercials for Burberry and McDonald's. That would be fine if it weren't for the case that McQueen's "artistry" is predicated on his fine-arts background and Loach wasn't the ghost of Trots past.

Conversely, the so-called whores are usually the ones with blue blood—and here we are, back with Sayadian and Borowczyk. Just like the Princess and the Pea, either of them is capable of singling out the lousy shot in a mountain of dailies. I'm not so sure about their peers. I'm not sure, for example, if there is such a thing as a lousy shot for someone like Zanussi.

It's a good time to be a fan of Stephen Sayadian's work.

First, Mitchell Froom's amazing soundtrack for Café Flesh just dropped[1]. It's a trippy ride in and of itself.

"I wanted it to sound like an Elmer Bernstein score from the '50s," Sayadian told Screen Slate's Jacqueline Castel[2], "only played with the most modern synthesizers available at the time. I thought: old vibe, new technology. And Mitch [Froom] was right on it, he understood."

Next up, though details are scant at the moment, Dr. Caligari is being released by Mondo Macabro this spring. (We might have mentioned that once or twice.)

Finally, audiences will be able to both see the film as it was meant to be seen *and finally hear* Jerry Stahl's incredible dialogue. The laser disc put out so long ago by the porn outfit Excalibur Films offered a muddy soundtrack that sank Stahl's verbal acrobatics underwater. This is no longer an issue.

A *Dr. Caligari* section would obviously be incomplete without a check-in[3] from director Sayadian himself.

So, here it is.

We like our artists to be introspective about their own work and life, with questions like, "Did you ever dream something you made in your youth would be so admired today?" With that in mind, how does it feel to finally see AND HEAR Dr. Caligari *the way you'd always intended?*

The real question is why was *Dr. Caligari* MIA for over 20 years? Originally released in 1989, it came out of the gate running, premiering at the Toronto Film Festival as the opening-night feature of the popular Midnight Madness

---

1   https://lightintheattic.net/releases/8393-cafe-flesh-original-motion-picture-soundtrack

2   Castel, Jacqueline. "The Music of Café Flesh." *Screen Slate*, www.screenslate.com/articles/music-cafe-flesh-soundtrack.

3   For previous Sayadian goodness, pick up *Exploitation Nation* #3 to read a full-length interview.

series. Jay Scott, Canada's top critic, gave it a glorious review, comparing it to Hitchcock, Buñuel, and Lynch. (Someone told me that Mr. Scott smoked a blunt before the screening. Whether it's true or not, I can't say, but it is an ideal way to watch the movie.[4])

Following Toronto, *Caligari* played at a number of art houses across the country, including the Nuart in L.A. and the 8th Street Playhouse in New York. Just about all the reviews were fantastic, even in the mainstream press.

Kevin Thomas of the *L.A. Times* called *Dr. Caligari* "the work of true visionaries." *New York Post* critic David Edelstein said, "...an hilarious satire, the lines themselves are out of Dada." *Entertainment Weekly*, not exactly known for being cutting edge, proclaimed *Dr. Caligari* "a newly minted cult classic."

After Toronto, L.A., and N.Y., it played midnight shows in Seattle, Dallas, Phoenix, San Francisco, Chicago, and Boston, plus a number of college campus theatres. It was even featured on MTV, which, at the time, was considered a very big deal.

Unfortunately, the company that financed the movie, Excalibur, had no experience in the motion-picture business, outside of selling X-rated video tapes. Even with all the great reviews, [Excalibur] had no idea how to market or promote the movie. Miraculously, they did turn a nice profit by selling both the foreign and videocassette rights. On a personal level, I have to admit that alone made me happy, as it continued my streak of always making money for my investors. Despite that bit of financial

---

4   It's true!

**A scene from *Dr. Caligari*. I dunno. Seems self-explanatory.
(All photos this section copyright and courtesy Stephen Sayadian.)**

success, by the mid-'90s, *Dr. Caligari* had pretty much disappeared.

SGE (Shapiro-Glickenhaus Entertainment), the L.A.-based company that owned and distributed the video tape, fell on hard times, eventually going out of business. That really hit me hard. I really liked the owners, and I know they were excited about our film. In fact, I was in preproduction talks with them about a new script Jerry Stahl and I had just completed called *Rapid Eye Movement*. Although the company specialized in action films, they also had a few oddities in their library, like *Frankenhooker*, which I believe they financed.

With SGE defunct, all the rights to *Caligari* returned to Excalibur. It wasn't long before they started selling the video (and later on, a no-frills DVD) through their mail-order catalog, alongside titles like *Anal Autopsy*, *The Little Spermaid*, and my personal fave, *They Call Her... Snuggle Bucket*. Thankfully, all of the film elements, including the original negative, sound reels, Mitchell Froom's soundtrack, etc., were carefully stored in the company vault. For over two decades, the film was ostensibly out of circulation. And yet, I never stopped believing it would eventually find its way back to me.

I knew *Caligari* had an audience, and once the internet started, the film began showing up on some very hip websites: Heather Drain/Mondo Heather, Tom Clark/Vortice Mortale, Yum-Yum/House of Self-Indulgence, Christopher S. Jordan/The Movie Sleuth, Tenebrous Kate, and many, many more. Even you wrote lovingly about *Caligari* in your *Movie Outlaw* series[5].

Following my liver transplant in 2007, I decided to try and buy the exclusive rights to *Caligari* myself. By then, Excalibur had a new owner, and trying to chase down the film and close the deal was nothing less than a quixotic clusterfuck. Finally, after 13 years, thanks to the heroic work of Daniel Bird and, later, Mondo Macabro's Pete Tombs, we finally made it happen.

Watching Acid Films' stunning restoration of *Dr. Caligari* at L.A.'s Beyond Fest was, to say the least, a dream come true...to say the most, a wet dream come true. The best part was watching it with cocreator/cowriter Jerry Stahl, along with Ladi von Jansky (DP) and Laura Albert (Mrs. Van Houten). The screening was completely sold out, yet the majority of the audience wasn't even born when we made the picture.

What surprised me most was, unlike the old days, not a single person walked out. Following the screening, Jerry, Ladi, Laura, and I did a Q&A. The entire audience remained in their seats—always a good sign—and bombarded us with really smart questions. After the official Q&A, we continued the jaw-wag in the lobby and, later, out in the street. On top of everything else, the film played in the same theater (Los Feliz) where we had our cast-and-crew screening 30 years ago. You couldn't write it any better.

Reading through the liner notes for the Café Flesh *soundtrack, I noticed*

---

5 It's true. I did write lovingly about *Dr. Caligari* in *Movie Outlaw: The Prequel*.

the word "subversion" comes up over and over again, not only with the intersection between porn, the kind of art you were doing, and the L.A. punk scene. Castel points out the shared resources between the Elfman clan and DEVO, somehow missing the Wall of Voodoo and Alex Cox faction (though not everyone can be mentioned). In addition, there's Stahl's edict to make "anti-porn." Is the subversion in your art nature or nurture? It seems you come by it honestly.

Definitely nature, and by a big mile. Subversion has always been the stepping-stone to my visuals. For me, it's not a gimmick, it is who I am. "He is great who is what he is from nature and who never reminds us of others." That's my mantra. Tip of the hat to Emerson.

With the older stuff finally being restored (and there's a wonderful infection spreading through the Blu-ray distributors, as a lot of indie folks are finally getting the recognition they deserve), do you want to talk at all about the future? Bird dropped hints toward Hell Is Tender being your masterpiece.

Our new film is called Hell Is Tender, a surreal fable about extreme devotion and eternal love. Although funny, warm, merciful and humane, it still manages to violate the laws of decency and canons of good taste. No easy task.

Keep checking Mondo Macabro for more information about Dr. Caligari: www.mondo-macabro.com.

You can also purchase all their past goodness here: Mondomacabro.bigcartel.com.

"Velkommen to Cafe Flesh."

Friday nights for an '80s kid meant a trip to the video store. For '80s kids like me, that meant a three-for-$5 weekend bargain on anything, new releases excluded. It's where a lot of us started, dreaming we'd have our own movies up there on the shelves someday.

Brad Sykes accomplished that goal as one of the last "first-wavers" (to use Andy Copp's scale of '80s to '90s as the "first wave" of indie filmmaking). Sykes's movies, particularly *Death Factory*, were staples of mom-and-pop video shelves. But the business is fluid, fickle, and mean as all hell. Fortunes came and went. Sykes, however, perseveres.

You were part of the first wave of indie filmmakers in the early '90s (if we start counting at Tim Ritter's 1986 film Truth or Dare?*). Was there a feeling of optimism starting out? Back in the home video days, a filmmaker could shoot a movie and actually get it picked up and seen by a real audience, which you had. What got you started, and what kept you going?*

When I was 15, I started shooting video shorts with my friends around my neighborhood. Later, I graduated to features—eight of them, to be exact—which I made during high school and college. During this time, I started reading *Film Threat Video Guide* (which gave me my first print review), *Alternative Cinema Magazine*, and John Russo's filmmaking books. I also rented movies like *Killing Spree*, *Shatter Dead*, and [Leif Jonker's] *Darkness*. It was very inspiring to see these regional movies made on lower budgets—but with a lot of heart and talent—and get real distribution, and it certainly encouraged me to continue along the path I'd been on.

I didn't expect to get to direct a "professional" movie so soon after moving to L.A. At the time, I was happy just working various crew and effects jobs. But the opportunity presented itself when a producer I had worked for saw a Hi-8 movie I had directed called *The Pact* and offered me the chance to make *Scream*

Queen, starring Linnea Quigley. It was a tough shoot and a real learning experience in terms of scheduling and working with crews, actors, etc. Nothing much happened with it, but it got me started as a professional, paid director. It wasn't until my third movie, *Camp Blood*, that I saw my movie on a shelf, got reviews (good and bad), and started having some real success as a filmmaker.

You built your cred early and often, with projects like Scream Queen, Death Factory *(with a young Tiffany Shepis), and* Camp Blood *(as an homage to the F13 films), and yet you're working under harsh conditions, with low budgets and tight schedules. How did the younger Brad Sykes view the film industry at this point? What was the highest highlight versus the lowest lowlight?*

Honestly, most of the time, I was just happy to be working and making a living directing horror, which is one of my favorite genres. On *Scream Queen*, obviously it was a real coup to have Linnea in the film, and working (and hanging out) with her was my favorite part of that experience. *Camp Blood* was a tough shoot for several reasons. We had weather to deal with, but we also had technical issues with the 3-D lens we were using.

Death Factory was even harder to make because although we had a location (a haunted attraction that was closed for the summer), there was no AC, running water, bathroom, etc., and almost no crew.

So, yes, the conditions were terrible. But, for me, the worst part wasn't the six-day shooting schedules or minimal resources, but the lack of production support, or, rather, the psychological abuse that occurred during those films. A lot of that was unwarranted and only hurt the film. Anyone who was there could attest to that, and those experiences were undoubtedly the lowlights of that period.

At the same time, *Camp Blood* and *Death Factory* ended up becoming two of my biggest hits and most well-known films. It was a real treat to see your work on the shelf, for rent or sale, and even being sold internationally. We made *Camp Blood 2* on the success of its U.K. sales alone, before the first one was even released in the U.S. That was pretty exciting in terms of how one movie's success could automatically translate into another opportunity.

One of my highlights during that period, though, was making a movie called *Mad Jack*, a *Hitcher*-style thriller I shot on 16mm in the Mojave Desert. Very few people have seen it, but it was a big accomplishment for me at the time, both professionally (I put the financing together) and creatively, as it was a spec I had written and pushed through the system. Once again, [it was] a very difficult shoot that pushed everyone involved to their limit…but the end result was very close to what I had envisioned. I'm still proud of that film.

Without disparaging too many of our peers, one thing that always stood out to me about your films is the tight, sometimes intricate stories, and (as I've found) you often have people instead of characters (and I mean that as a good thing). Did you ever get blowback for writing something or get told to "dumb it down"? Do you have a process? Did a film ever come before the script? (For example, we've written movies around locations.)

Well, thank you! I've always tried to write the most original scripts I could, with scenes and characters I hadn't seen before, regardless of the budget, the schedule, and other parameters. I truly enjoy the process, whatever the budget/project is. I write most of my movies myself and still do a lot of outside writing work, so I've always been a writer first, director second.

Some movies I have written or at least pitched as specs, meaning I wrote them and then took the projects around to investors. Those films (like *Mad Jack*, *Demon's Kiss*, *Goth*, and *Plaguers*) are usually the ones I end up being most satisfied with. On others, I was presented with a title or idea—in one case, just a poster—and hired to write the script. *Death Factory* was one of those. So, you try and make it your own and, like you said, make it feel as believable as possible.

I've never really had to dumb anything down, but I have had plenty of creative interference or parameters to deal with. On *Witchcraft XII*, for

(All photos courtesy and copyright Brad Sykes.)

example (and probably others I did for Vista Street), there had to be a sex scene every so many minutes/pages. So, then you try and make those scenes connect to the plot in some way, or at least serve some dramatic purpose. The funny thing is, on that one, I must have written too many sex scenes, as they ended up cutting one out. You just can't win with some people!

As far as a process goes, whether I'm writing around an existing location or not, I always write a treatment first to see if there's a movie there, with one page equaling roughly 10 pages of script. I wouldn't go into preproduction without at least an 80-page script, or else you risk the film coming up too short. Apart from that, every script is different in terms of pacing, structure, etc.

One thing I've always tried to do as a writer and director, even now, is go a bit beyond one's budgetary limitations, which I think every filmmaker, especially indie filmmakers, must do to make a memorable film. If you don't, I just don't see the point.

One highlight had to have been working with Steve Railsback on Plaguers. *Any great Steve stories? You've worked with folks on all ends of the Hollywood spectrum. Do the A-listers or A-minus-listers require more attention or care?*

That was a career highlight, and it was a real pleasure working with Steve. When I was writing *Plaguers*, I did something I usually never do, which is to write a character with a specific actor in mind. But that time, I did, and lo and behold, my wife and producer, Josephina, tracked him down…and he said yes! I'll never forget the first time he called us at home; the first time I heard his voice on the phone, it was kind of surreal. Steve later told me that the only other time a writer wrote a character for him was Chris Carter with "Duane Barry" from *The X-Files*.

As you know, one of Steve's best films is *The Stunt Man*. I had told him I was a big fan of the film and must have mentioned that I didn't have a copy of the (then-new) Anchor Bay DVD.

So, one day, Steve had a long break in the middle of the shooting day and left. When he came back, he had bought me the deluxe DVD of *The Stunt Man*, which he autographed and inscribed to me, saying some very flattering things. That pretty much stopped me in my tracks.

One of the coolest things about Steve was how much he loves

L–R: Brad Sykes, Josephina Sykes, and Steve Railsback from *Plaguers*

filmmaking and has such enthusiasm after all these years. I hope I can say the same thing when I'm his age.

I've worked with other stars, like C. Thomas Howell and Danielle Harris, and from my experience, they're not divas and don't necessarily need anything more than a director or producer who knows what they're doing and can guide them through the film. Once they trust you, they'll follow you anywhere.

Over the years, the industry has taken a strange turn. While it should be a paradise for indie filmmakers now, with streaming services abounding, it's still difficult to get work seen and paid for—and if you land the former, the latter is always way off. How have you managed to adapt to what can be legitimately seen as a purge of indie content?

You bring up a very good point, and one that I've been discussing with other veterans a lot lately. There's way too much stuff out there, and in streaming, unlike the video shelf, titles are easily lost in the shuffle, especially since there's way more horror out there from bigger companies like Blumhouse and A24 that seem to garner all the attention.

Personally, my response to this is to try and do fewer films, make them as high-quality and personal as possible, and not try to follow any trends. I don't see the point of just chucking stuff out into the marketplace for a quick buck…if there is such a thing anymore.

That's why we made Hi-8: Horror Independent 8 back in 2013. I needed to recharge my batteries and do something small and completely

independent after spending so much time in development on various "bigger" films that went nowhere. And other participating filmmakers were also excited to make something that they had total creative control over. We spent very little on it to minimize financial risk and just had fun, like in the old days. The funny thing is, Hi-8 ended up doing very well and garnering a lot of attention and positive reviews—some of the best reviews of my career, in fact. We played over 20 fests and even got a nice retro VHS release. I still hear from people who enjoyed it. There's a lesson there, somewhere.

Tell us a bit about the current project, Hi-Fear.

Hi-Fear is the third and final chapter in the franchise that began with Hi-8. On the second film, Hi-Death, we got "bigger" in terms of formats and storytelling, and in *Hi-Fear*, we've encouraged all the filmmakers to explore their deepest fears. The four directors involved in *Hi-Fear* are Tim Ritter, Todd Sheets (*Dreaming Purple Neon*), Anthony Catanese (*Girls Just Wanna Have Blood*), and me. Tim, Todd, and I have directed segments for all three movies in the series, and it's been really cool collaborating with these guys who inspired me back in the day. The movie is in the final stages of post now and will be finished soon. All I can say is, if you liked the other two films or are a fan of the filmmakers' other movies, you'll enjoy *Hi-Fear*. We've saved the best for last!

We older folks seem to be enjoying a resurgence of sorts, with outfits like Vinegar Syndrome lining up to restore our older projects. Are any restorations of your films on the horizon? Anything on the wish list?

Three of my older films—*Scream Queen*, *Evil Sister 2* (a sequel in name only that mixes road movie and Eurohorror), and *Bewitching* (also known as *B-Witched*, starring Shana Lane-Block from *Who's the Boss?* and *Blackout*)—all of them rare and long OOP (out of print), currently have a home with Visual Vengeance, a sister label of Wild Eye Releasing, which will be releasing special editions at some point in the future. I put the extras together for them a while ago, and [the films will] be coming out throughout the year.

Keep up with Brad Sykes's adventures at: www.facebook.com/Nightfallpix/.

Brad and Linnea Quigley

NO MORE WAITING. HERE'S CHARLES PINION

"Charles Pinion is untypical of the majority of the New Wave Horror Movie makers. [...] Unlike the majority of his peers he has not adopted the persona of the stereotypical genre movie director. In truth he acts more like an artist or musician (in the real sense) and if anything is a little too self-critical. However he is amongst the most exciting and daring filmmakers working in the underground today. Like Jim Van Bebber, his movies owe as much to the Cinema of Transgression as they do the 70s horror movie boom. His films are also less to do with the traditions of the genre than with true-life horror. Yet, where Van Bebber uses hallucination and dream for what they are, Pinion manages to sustain that dream/unreal quality throughout the entire running time of a movie without confusing or deterring from the narrative. Indeed, unlike most film makers dabbling in 'art driven' (read: self-indulgent), who linger on shocking or symbolic imagery as a means of 'expanding' (read padding out) the 'unconventional' (read: lack of) narrative, Charles Pinion's filmmaking is very economical; so much so that We Await clocks in at a mere 58 mins yet loses nothing in either the horror or artistic impacts."
— Richard King, 2002

In 2002, I was working for *Film Threat* and *Femme Fatales* as a struggling journalist, hobbing knobs with many influential and ambitious indie filmmakers, when I was employed to edit a book about these fine young cannibals , written by legendary U.K. distributor Richard King. To jog your memory, King was at the center of the Video Nasties hysteria that gripped Great Britain in the '80s and '90s. A lot of cool folks got caught up in that, our own Scooter McCrae among them.

King's book, originally titled *Video Massacre*, was filled with interviews with such folks as Scooter, Tim (*Truth or Dare?*) Ritter, J.R. (*The Dead Next Door*) Bookwalter, Brinke Stevens, Kevin Lindenmuth—so many of the first-wave-of-indie-horror folks, the first ones to really embrace the

Punk rock meets indie DIY, as it always has. (All photos this section courtesy and copyright Charles Pinion.)

home video market. This early list also includes Charles Pinion, and shamefully, the experience described above was my introduction to his work.

From his first film, Twisted Issues, to present day, Pinion has embodied a signature style that blends imagery and punk rock spirit, a style that sets him apart from many of his first-wave fellows. Working with one foot in punk music and the other in pornography (under the pseudonym Charley Crow[1]), Pinion makes films that tell tight, horrific stories with a gleeful sadism reminiscent of the

---

[1] The Charley Crow porn films, particularly the 1988 offering *Archer's Last Day* (featuring porn legend Tom Byron) and the marvelously titled *Cornhole Armageddon* (1995), showcase the same bizarre sensibilities as *Red Spirit Lake* and *We Await*. It puts one in mind of Vernon Chatman's *Final Flesh* or the anti-porn of Stephen Sayadian.

Cinema of Transgression aesthetic spearheaded by Richard Kern, Nick Zedd, Lydia Lunch, et al. In point of fact, Kern costars in Pinion's *Red Spirit Lake*, his energy a perfect match for the gonzo narrative.

Red Spirit Lake and *We Await* are the two titles synonymous with Pinion. Both are awash with the requisite sex and gore and accompanied by bizarre, surreal, dreamlike, and nightmarish imagery. A dog-man humps a captive. A gargantuan Jesus attempts to eat a station wagon full of murderers. Spirits that transcend good and evil play a vicious game with humanity. Pinion's movies are profane, hilarious, and grotesque. So, of course, there's a lot to recommend.

"I think they stand up fine as artifacts of their time and the process of their making," says Pinion. "Both movies are deep collaborations and thus bear the scars of creativity and human frailty. Ultimately, both movies make me smile, and I am proud of them as my imperfect children."

Was there a feeling of optimism when you began making Twisted Issues? *Back in the home video days, a filmmaker could shoot a movie and actually get it picked up and seen by a real audience, which you had. What got you started, and what kept you going?*

I'll be honest. *Twisted Issues* came out of the DIY, punk rock, "fuck conventional-goal-orientation-and-careerism" gestalt of the time. I came from a fine-arts background (as a painter and printmaker at Syracuse University), so I was aggressively noncommercial from the get-go. My punk band, Psychic Violents, was similarly uninterested in pursuing "success" (though we would have welcomed it). *Twisted Issues* was meant to be a document of the Gainesville, Florida, music scene initially, but it evolved into the psycho-punk splatter-comedy it eventually became. I never anticipated selling it, and I had no idea that the movie would later be emblematic of the shot-on-video movement.

There is definitely a connection between [punk and indie filmmaking], at least from my perspective. Part of my motivation in shooting movies on video was its intrinsic pugnacity toward established norms. The "rules" were made to be broken. Having said that, there's always an argument for "artotainment," which writer-filmmaker-musician John Skipp abbreviates "entertaining art."

Twisted Issues was also intended to be the final chapter in a series of art zines I'd made: *Twisted Tissues Sputtering*, *Twisted Tissues Too*, *Twisted Tissues Tales for Teens*, *Twisted Tissues Special Caffeine Edition*, and *Twisted Tissues Fun-Time Poster* (and the never-completed *Twisted Tissues Six*). *Twisted Issues* never got any kind of legitimate release. I sold it by mail on VHS for $15 postpaid, in a large Ziploc bag with the 90-minute soundtrack cassette and a little booklet. *Film Threat* put it on the map by featuring it in their "20 Underground Films You MUST See!" issue.

Up until a few years ago, the winning formula for indie horror was "gore plus nudity plus don't overthink it." The story and characters were often incidental. But so many of us—you included—found ways of getting substance into the films. For instance, as with Shatter Dead, Red Spirit Lake's *sex and nudity is actually motivated by the story. Did you feel constricted, or were you eager to get into the skin and blood?*

With *Twisted Issues*, I made the movie to be seen on the 12-inch Sony Trinitron that my character watches during the movie. So, it was important for me to have a high BSI,

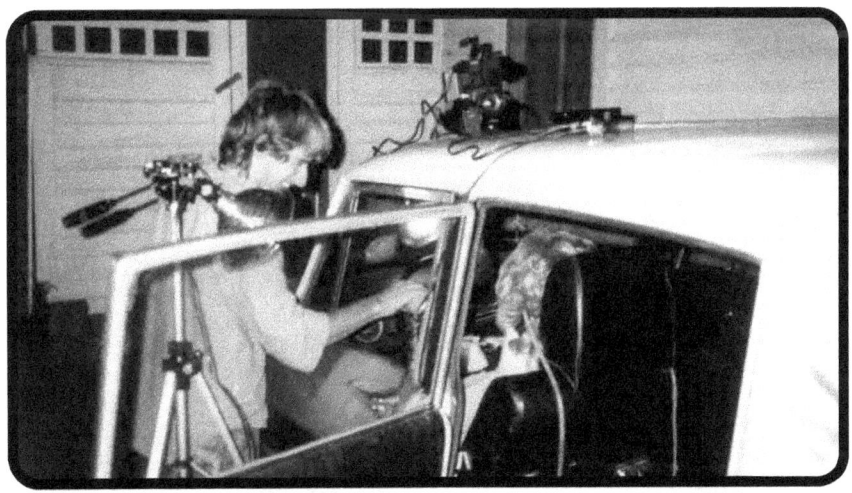

Behind the scenes on *Twisted Issues* (All photos this section courtesy and copyright Charles Pinion. All Rights Reserved.)

which was my initialism for "blood per square inch" of screen. (Greg Ceton, who played guitar in the band Just Demigods on the soundtrack, assumed it stood for "blood saturation index," which isn't bad either.)

Because I'm a painter, color was super important to me, and red is a stimulating color, so I felt it important to have a lot of it on the screen.

Nudity is noticeably lacking in *Twisted Issues*. In fact, when I first met Richard Kern, he commented that, watching it, he kept waiting for one of the girls to take her top off.

It wasn't until *Red Spirit Lake* and the influence of my collaborator Ellen Smithy that I really embraced on-screen transgressive sexuality as an aesthetic of its own. I had also quit Al Goldstein's *Screw Magazine* shortly before making *Red Spirit Lake*, so I'm sure I carried some of that publication's sexual energy and irreverence with me. (Rick Hall [the bald, screaming bad guy who meets a bad end in the snow in *Red Spirit Lake*] and David Aaron Clark [the giant Jesus in *We Await*] both worked at *Screw* when I did.)

Care to talk about your time at Screw?

I started working for Al Goldstein's cable show, *Midnight Blue*. It was on the fourth floor of the building on W 14th (*Screw Magazine* was upstairs on the eleventh floor). I made a couple of cool videos there (one was called "I Get Ideas," which had a classic crooner's version of the song with images from *Häxan, The Devils, Videodrome, Broadway Melody of 1936*, and others). It was why I was hired at the time, to

Underground artist Mike Diana's cover for *We Await* (For more on Diana, check out *ExNat* #6.)

liven up the show. Of course, I spent a lot of time taking a video camera up to various restaurants or stores that had done Al wrong, where I would shoot exteriors and B-camera for his "Fuck You" segment of the show. *Midnight Blue* was a groundbreaker in the free-cable world.

Eventually, there was an opening up there, and I got hired as a paste-up guy (back when you actually pasted text and images to "boards" for publication). It's where I met David Aaron Clark, who had an office next to mine. So many great artists and other creative types walked through those doors. It's where I met Danny Hellman, Dale Ashmun, Kevin Hein, and so many others. There was a triumvirate of *High Times Magazine*, *Screw*, and the WFMU radio station that created a nexus of creative energy. (*High Times* did a great review of *Twisted Issues*, with color photos and so on, which was a first for me!)

It wasn't until I moved to Los Angeles a decade later that I started shooting and editing adult material as Charley Crow. Under that name, I wrote and directed four adult titles before leaving the business.

Pinion and *We Await* co-writer Ellen Smithy

Over the years, the industry has taken a strange turn. How have you managed to adapt to what can be legitimately viewed as a purge of indie content?

Truthfully, I am a working stiff at a 9-to-5 job these days. I'm not really involved in the filmmaking business much. I am, however, currently collaborating on a screenplay with a coworker, so we shall see where that goes. I still have some stories to tell (e.g., *Thousand Eyes* and *Dimension Door*), and I hope someday to tell them. I will probably do so in the way I always have: for an extremely small budget and with the participation of friends. And I'd like to shoot them myself, probably on a camcorder.

Not to keep hammering away at the ravages of linear time, but how do you feel as an older filmmaker compared to how you felt as a younger artist? How have you grown? Is there anything you think you used to do better?

Oh, there's an energy deficit for sure. I made *Twisted Issues* in the same time period I was driving a cab from 6 p.m. to 6 a.m. and washing dishes in a diner. Yet somehow, I had the energy and enthusiasm to make that movie! Most importantly, I had an energetic circle of friends and collaborators, which made all the difference. In a future production, I want to shoot it myself again, and again work with devoted friends.

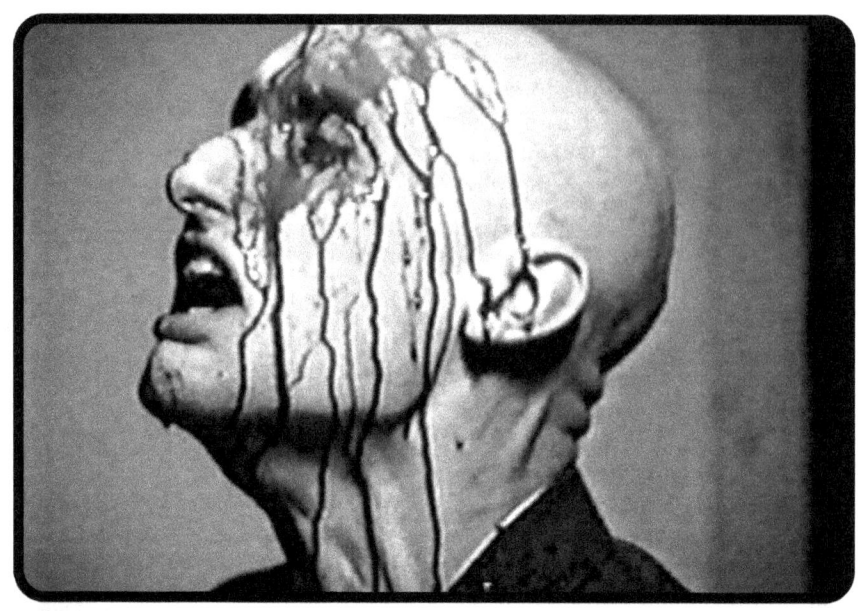

A bloody Rick Hall in *Red Spirit Lake*

Building on the above, how was working on Try Again?[2]

It was fun. My friend Adam wrote and starred in it, and my girlfriend, Jeannine, produced it. The biggest expense was the effects guy, which Adam insisted on (and paid for). I could have told the same story with ketchup squirting out, and it would have worked for me.

What was the best day of filmmaking you had on Red Spirit Lake?

Oh, wow. *Red Spirit Lake* had so many good days. I really enjoyed the day we shot Rick Hall's death scene out in the snow. In order to get those spinning shots of Rick "dancing" with the witches, I tied a rope around our respective waists, and we spun around and around, eventually falling down every time. We did a few takes. That sort of spur-of-the-moment problem-solving is part of the fun of "availablist" (Kembra Pfahler's term) art-making. Doing it while you're freezing your ass off in the snow (Of course, Rick was eventually naked) just made it more satisfying. Meanwhile, the sauna was available to recuperate in between takes.

Red Spirit Lake and *We Await* just got a snazzy rerelease on a double-feature Blu-ray thanks to Saturn's Core. The Charles Pinion double feature is rife with extras and a beefy liner-note booklet boasting a Pinion interview conducted by Mike Hunchback. See the review on page 54.

---

2   Included on the Saturn's Core double-feature Blu-ray release of *Red Spirit Lake* and *We Await*, Pinion's short film *Try Again* is a charming little story about the frustrating pitfalls of suicide.

BY TiM RittER

At the end of 2020, I was having dinner with producer Al Nicolosi, a friend of mine from the 1980s. Al and I started making movies together in 1985. A couple of years later, we made the film *Killing Spree* together and, by the end of the production, had a huge falling out due to "creative differences." In 2020, some 33 years later, we had just reunited and collaborated on a new movie, *Sharks of the Corn*, for SRS Cinema.

Al was probably 26 years old, and I was a 16-year-old high-schooler, when we were first best friends. By 1985, all of my pals were in their 20s or 30s, because I wanted to make movies, and I couldn't do that without cool adults who also wanted to make independent movies. I had little use for the partying high school kids my own age. Another great friend was Vincent Miranda, then in his 30s. He knew H.G. Lewis (!), ghostwrote Scholastic horror movie books and articles, hung out with George Romero, and worked on many South Florida indie movies, like *Shock Waves*.

Vince gave me a copy of the Romero *Day of the Dead* script that was set on the island (before the project was cut down in size for budgetary reasons). This was in 1984, before the movie had rolled!

At 16, with my *Day of the Reaper* Super 8mm feature completed and selling to video stores, I felt like I was officially "in the biz" and on the road to great success. I introduced Al to Vince, and I also dragged another good friend into the mix: Joel D. Wynkoop, who was well into his 20s and a filmmaking mentor, friend, and former neighbor (and my babysitter a decade prior). Joel wanted to be an actor and had tried to go out to Hollywood at one point (with $300 and no plan in mind), but his car broke down on the way and he never made it (so I was told). He ended up back in Florida, working at Kmart and a furniture-moving company, and we reconnected when his nephew saw an ad for my *Day of the Reaper* feature in the high school newspaper. Together, we sold Beta and VHS copies of *Day*

L–R: Tim Ritter and Al Nicolosi (All photos this section copyright and courtesy Tim Ritter.)

of the Reaper to mom-and-pop video stores up and down Florida in what I saw as the opportunity of a lifetime: to have my "awesome" movies seen by the public, rented at stores!

Al, Joel, Vince, and I set out to make a SOV VHS anthology movie called Twisted Illusions, inspired by Creepshow and The Twilight Zone. (Lofty ambitions?) Al worked for an ABC affiliate at Master Control and had his own video production company, Video Events. I ended up hanging out with Al during midnight shifts at his job, taking it all in, and working at his production company, learning how to shoot, edit, and master on video. With my Super 8 film experience, it wasn't too difficult. We shot weddings, documentaries, commercials, and all kinds of things. Asbestos Felt, who worked with Al at the TV station, would join us in the commercial video work. Later, he acted in three of our first features, including Killing Spree!

I started making movies with the family homemade Super 8 camera in 1978, so I've been making films in some capacity now, ceaselessly, for over 44 years! Writing books, ideas, and scripts and making them into movies or video movies is something I have just...always done, instinctively, like I had no choice. I have never felt any other calling, really, or *wanted* to do anything else whatsoever.

Fast-forward to the dinner with Al in October 2020, at which time we were finishing up Sharks of the Corn and celebrating at a fancy restaurant. Over exquisite food and fine wine, Al asked me a serious question. He had left the movie business after our personal Killing Spree fiasco to become a successful financial investor and had made a nice life for himself. The movie bug had remained with him, so he'd continued to work on ideas here and there, and he'd acted in plays and such when possible, but he had not pursued the madness like he and I had with dogged determination between 1984 and 1989 or so.

Now, I had continued making movies through the ups and downs of life after Killing Spree. I just couldn't stop. Even if I couldn't raise money for a budget, I'd shoot something, with budgets ranging from $350 to $350,000. Most of the time, I'd use any residuals I got for the project, or I'd put them into the next movie idea to keep rolling.

So, in addition to making movies, I would work regular jobs (for instance, a security job on the night shift, so I could work on movies during the day [and never sleep!]). Sometimes, I worked two jobs at once: as a youth director for a civic center and as an assistant manager at a mom-and-pop video store, while trying to make and sell my own independent horror movies. There were extreme ups and downs, and my wife, Kathy, willingly went with me on the obsessive journey of making indie movies first and foremost, before anything else... as long as we could pay the bills. She would help me assemble props, schedule things, and do special effects. She also jumped in and played any part she had to when someone wouldn't show up, something for which I'm forever grateful. And she got quite good at acting!

At the big meal with Al, he asked me the question: "Do you have any regrets? You know, any regrets about the path you took, just forging ahead and making movie after movie, after over 30 years of struggling?"

"Regrets?" I thought. Hmm. I flashed back to a lot of crazy moments.

I remembered doing open auditions for *Twisted Illusions* at a 45th Street motel back in 1985. Joel and I had put flyers on cars at shopping mall parking lots to spread the "word of mouth"—like everyone wanted to be an actor! We had maybe three people show up to read for a part until these two prostitutes noticed us sitting in a room with the door open and a video camera sitting on a tripod and decided they wanted to audition for a movie. What happened from there probably should stay on 45th Street history!

Then, there was the time Al and I went to pick up Joel to edit *Twisted Illusions*. We got to his apartment parking lot, and there Joel went, lying on the hood of his car, swishing past us in reverse, hanging on like Clint Eastwood in *Magnum Force*, fingers gripping the front hood edge while someone navigated his car out at full speed, his car screeching off toward a flatbed pickup truck nearby. It was the repo man, and Joel was trying to stop his car from being taken, action movie style. Needless to say,

Tim of the Corn meets shark.

Where the first wave of indie horror got started

it didn't work. Joel was always having trouble reconciling bills during our moviemaking period, until he got a steady job delivering water in the 1990s.

Later, when Al, Joel, Vince, and I got a $250,000 budget for *Truth or Dare? A Critical Madness*, based on one of the most popular shorts in *Twisted Illusions*, we were all systematically cut from the project due to producer and investor interference. It was a trial by fire, a film-school-as-you-go kind of epic experience in learning and humiliation. Joel was cut as the leading man and reduced to a cameo. Al, who had produced the movie up until we filmed, was cut out as producer and ended up just shooting a behind-the-scenes documentary on the making of the movie, which I had to pay him for out of my "salary." Vince was an assistant director who ended up being cut down to assistant cameraman, though he was later relieved of those duties.

When the producers found out I was 17 years old when I wrote the script and signed the contract to make *Truth or Dare? A Critical Madness* (midway through the shoot), everyone took sides, and it became a war of wills to get the movie completed. The head honcho did everything he could to get rid of me and make my life miserable, even as every decision he had made on the production seemed to fail: Makeup men didn't deliver what they promised, we kept running out of money, the "dailies" didn't arrive until days after we shot, the production schedule had omitted shooting key sequences.... On and on the list went, with me in the middle, determined that this would be the first direct-to-video horror film to hit the national markets! (We were close, but a few movies beat us to the punch because of all the dissension on our film.) But I was determined to finish the movie at any cost.

One of my worst memories of *Truth or Dare?* (apart from the time I got mad at a producer and was pounding on his hotel room door like a madman, trying to break it down to confront him—before my dad and Joel pulled me away from the splintered door) was when we shot the sequence where actor John Brace tries to stab his ex-wife, played by Mary Fanaro, in a kitchen. We shot at a North Palm Beach home about 15 miles from the production hotel. After constantly having to discreetly redirect every scene after it was blocked wrong by meddling producers, I helped the crew pack up when we were done, and somehow, I got left behind at the location! I ended up having to walk back to the hotel in the middle of a cold January night, when it was in the 30s in Florida and I didn't have a jacket. It was a very aggravating experience, that they thought so little of me as "director" and deliberately left me behind. I'll never forget that long, infuriating, four-hour walk back to the hotel.

The *Truth or Dare?* shoot got so bad that when we couldn't afford to film a scene the way it was written, or when the special effects weren't ready and we had to change everything, I'd just smugly tell the producers, "Fine, fine, I'll use this idea in my next movie"…which I did. Many of the *Killing Spree* gags were unused ideas from *Truth or Dare?* Then, there was the time we shot a car crash with stunt men, and one of the cars rammed into a utility pole we hadn't seen in the trees, blowing up the transformer and taking out electricity for the community of houses behind it, including the town mayor's pad! He was more than upset with me!

Killing Spree…there are great memories there too! We got kicked out of a church office where we were holding auditions for the main part of a nymphomaniac housewife, and the subsequent scandal hit the local press with a vengeance: *"Pornographers Casting Movie in Local Church!"*

We also got kicked out of Al's house (the main location) mid-shoot due to all the blood and destruction we were causing. Later on set, after 23 hours of shooting, Vince Miranda got so mad at Al that he just screamed at him at the top of his lungs in the living room and chased him outside into the backyard, where they got into a scuffle!

When I manned the counters at a mom-and-pop video store in the '90s, there was nothing quite like renting your own movie out to the casual, discriminating renter in those days. Most of our customers didn't know I had made *Killing Spree*, so it was quite the chore hearing uncensored feedback directly. *"Can I have a refund on this piece of garbage? My kid could make a better movie than this with our camcorder. I've never seen something so sloppy, pathetic, and not entertaining. We fast-forwarded through practically the whole thing! You all shouldn't carry low-end stuff like this and make us think it's a REAL movie. What were you thinking? I wanna refund!"* I'd decline

the refund, of course, also making a mental note that the other tape they returned was from the back room of the store (the Adult room) and was called *Bi-Bi American Style*. "I wonder how the production value was ON THAT," I'd think.

Shattered but too stupid to stop, I spent years trying to raise money for *Truth or Dare 2*, which became a $12,000 video movie called *Wicked Games*. My memories of making *Wicked Games* are overall pretty good despite having to shoot the movie twice due to analog tape issues. Shooting the infamous sprinkler murder scene, though, was a nightmare. While it was exciting filming a topless sunbather (Lori Zippo) being impaled on a sprinkler that then turns on and gushes out blood, shooting the scene was a chore, especially getting those low angles. The backyard was full of unshoveled dog crap, both fresh and probably dating back some 20 years. I didn't realize it until too late. Yes, there was the putrid smell, but wow, when I lay down to get those low angles, my light jeans got covered with feces—smeared, ruined! The entire lawn was nothing but animal feces no matter where you stepped (or lay)—hard, soft, crunchy, brittle, mashed into the mud.... It was all over my arms, the camera, the tripod, my tank top, my chest.... Poor Lori had to lie down in it too (Although, now that I think about it, we might've used a little cement patio for the blood-gushing shot), but she was not happy either! It was definitely a crappy day getting that footage on the tape!

Later, I'd go to war with Palm Beach County when it tried to legally snatch all the *Wicked Games* raw footage that

Tim with Stacey Savage, lead singer of the band Savage Master.

had been shot on public beaches, because I "didn't have a film permit or a million-dollar insurance policy." I went on a local cable TV show and discussed the issue. Pretty soon, the scandal spread all over Florida, from Miami to Orlando, and was even picked up by national newspapers as "the unfriendly indie film atmosphere Florida is showing its local filmmakers." I even got my own 900-number hotline, where people could listen to the comments I had made about the Florida Film Commission on the TV show, comments that were later edited out by the county for "painting a negative picture"! It did, however, boost the visibility of an otherwise very obscure SOV movie.

Making movies in Florida had become a constant source of turmoil and depression for me, but on I went! Another low point was doing a radio show with H.G. Lewis and having him completely trash-talk *Killing Spree* live on the air, saying that my effects looked fake (!) and the writing and story were pure nonsense, unlike his own horror masterpieces. Here I was, meeting an idol—someone who had inspired me from the beginning—and he was treating me like garbage needing to be thrown out for all to hear. Driving home after the interview, I broke down in tears of defeat, embarrassment, and humiliation, vowing to quit making movies altogether.

An article in the [South Florida] *Sun-Sentinel* on *Wicked Games* led to Kathy Willets contacting me and wanting to be in my next movie, whatever it was! So, naturally, I said, "Sure!" After going national with her bizarre story, Kathy had become a

Scream queen Michelle Macabre

scandalous celebrity in South Florida. She had charged men for sex, and her cop husband, Jeff, decided not only to get off on the events by watching from the closet, but to videotape it all so they could get off on it later. Among Kathy's clientele had been policemen, town officials, and a Broward County mayor! Naturally, when the story broke, it was very scandalous, with lots of graphic video evidence. Kathy had claimed that being on the antidepressant Prozac had made her "too horny to stop," and the rest of it went on and on. She and Jeff ended up doing jail time for prostitution, illegal wiretapping (that pesky videocam mic), and other things. When she and

L–R: Director Tim Ritter, actress Katrina, actor Jason Boyd, and in the foreground, actress/makeup FX artist Shannon Stockin

Jeff got out, Kathy was on the road to becoming a stripper, porno star, and adult entertainer, with a boob job that, well...was very noticeable! Her bust size was 80 (37FF), which male fans couldn't get enough of. She was also a regular on the celebrity circuit TV show trail, appearing on programs like *A Current Affair* and *Geraldo*. She agreed to publicize my movie on those venues. So, naturally, I cast her in a movie I wrote called *Creep*, in which she plays a battered stripper and prostitute who goes on a killing spree with her psycho brother, Angus (played by Joel Wynkoop).

Kathy was great to collaborate with and was a hard worker. We didn't shy away from shooting full-on, Jess Franco-style nudity and sex, some right in the woods right off I-95, in broad daylight! It was an insane time. We also shot at the notorious T's Lounge strip club in West Palm Beach, where Kathy had been busted doing a "sexually lewd" stage show in which she masturbated with a flashlight, turning it on and off with her vagina muscles (so customers could "see deep inside her"). Naturally, I decided to recreate this magic moment in the movie in the same club where she had been busted, at the same time the court trial was beginning!

When the press got wind of what we were doing, they had a field day, of course. All this went national thanks to the local tabloid TV shows, and it was an incredible, whirlwind experience for me, being covered everywhere as we filmed. Most of my family just watched in red-faced shame, shaking their heads in disbelief during the last few months of 1995. I really felt like we had "made it" with this one! One night, we shot a prostitution-slaughter sequence inspired by the crimes of Danny Rolling at a hotel room, and things got completely out of control in a *Caligula: The Untold Story* type of way! Joe D'Amato would've been proud, right?

One of my wackiest memories of *Creep* was scouting the local strip clubs for talent and locations and going in to see these live dancers for the first time. I remember going into a fancy gentlemen's club and watching the gals, mesmerized, trying to find areas to film our script amidst the flashing, colorful Argento lights and shapely female curves blinking on and off at me from the semidarkness. Finding a leather couch "back area" for private dances, I quickly called producer Michael Ornelas over so that I could show him the perfect area where we could shoot a conversation between our leads. I leaned back, my hands sliding across the upholstery, and suddenly, I found my palms engulfed in a massive puddle of sperm that had been ejaculated all over the cushion! I looked at it in open-mouthed disbelief as Mike laughed his head off.

When the local newspapers got wind that Tim Ritter and Joel Wynkoop were teaming up with "local hooker Kathy Willets," and the articles were accompanied by a picture of Joel holding a machete to Kathy's throat as she sported an orgasmic look on her face, the newspapers faced severe criticism and mass cancellations, and I got a ton of death threats for spearheading the project!

Interest in *Creep* was high, and I self-distributed again on VHS. I was so excited when an 18-wheeler semi-trailer truck backed up to my apartment and delivered a pallet full of *Creep* tapes that I had presold! It was thousands of copies! I mailed them out COD (cash on delivery) to locations all over the U.S. during the ensuing weeks, failing to check the box that eliminated checks as a cool way to pay. Within a month, dozens and dozens of bounced checks were coming home to Poppy! Tapes that had not been paid for had been mailed, distributed, and sent to stores, and after a hurricane pounded the east coast of Florida in the summer of 1995, I was in debt up to my eyes. I tried to file a suit against the distributors for mail fraud, but when the powers that be found out it was for a "Kathy Willets porn movie," no lawyer would help me, and the state refused to assist (even threatening anyone who tried to help me), because Kathy was on a blacklist for bringing down politicians and local rich men. She had also recently beat the lewd and lascivious lawsuit the state had brought against her. In no time at all, I had become a "gorenographer" and public enemy no. 1. There was no cool 900-number for me this time around, not even a dirty one!

The worst moment was when my accountants told me I had to pay state taxes on all the tapes I had sold, even though I'd received no payment from anyone for them—but I was personally responsible for paying the taxes on merchandise that had been stolen from me! Once again, I swore it was time to quit this madness, that there was no way to win in the moviemaking game.

But no, I didn't stop. I went on to make movies that got us shot at, busted by the cops, chased after by politicians, harassed by the public,

crucified by the press, and even threatened and intimidated by collaborators! I never knew what to expect every time I took out my video camera...other than trouble with a capital T!

While filming the ultra-sleazy *Screaming for Sanity* at our main location (an old hotel in Fort Pierce), we had to endure giant wharf rats that ran through the ceilings and rooms the entire time, stealing our pizza catering anytime we left it unattended! I'm not sure what customers thought of that when they checked in, but soon after we filmed there, the whole place was condemned, torn down, and leveled to make way for a new building.

Dirty Cop No Donut was guerilla moviemaking at its finest, as we basically just showed up anywhere without warning, with or without actors, and unleashed Joel as a psycho, egotistical cop doing what he wanted within the confines of the story, and after things played out, we'd sign up people and locations if they were cool with it! It wasn't exactly the best way to do things, and I surely wouldn't recommend it in our current day and age! But in 1996, 1997...it seemed like the way to pull this one off, wildly inspired by David Szulkin's *Making of [The Last House on the Left]* book and TV's *Cops*, giving a middle finger to the world as we went! Ah, to be an angry young man with "artistic visions"....

Moving up to Kentucky, I wrote a couple of books and continued to crank out video movies while working odd jobs. I made a movie called *Reconciled* with Larry Joe Treadway, which went incredibly smoothly, returning to the Christian roots of my childhood (an exorcism of sorts compared to the debauchery of *Creep* and *Screaming for Sanity*). I also made *Twisted Illusions 2, Deadly Dares: Truth or Dare IV, Hi-8 (Horror Independent 8), Hi-Fear, I Dared You! Truth or Dare V* (with *Ghost Hunters International* star Scott Tepperman), and more recently, *Sharks of the Corn*, reuniting me with Al and allowing me to collaborate with actress/FX artist Shannon Stockin. I'm also working on a new anthology movie with Donald Farmer called *Catnado*, of all the oddball things.

"Regrets?" I pondered again at that meal with Al in 2020, chewing a big hunk of meat and then swallowing. "No. Not really. No regrets. I don't think I would change a thing with my choices. This is the only time...*I really feel alive!*"

Afterword: I rang in 2022 with Vinegar Syndrome and Terror Vision Video Records and Video, releasing a deluxe Blu-ray of *Killing Spree* with a limited-edition slipcover. So, things are still moving forward! Although I still struggle financially, I'm ecstatic that *Killing Spree* has received the honor of being released by one of the biggest boutique horror/exploitation labels in the business (and that I don't have to mail the copies out myself). Like the article published in *Fangoria* #146 that covered all of my movies up until then, this latest achievement gives me the feeling of winning an Academy Award, so...what can I say? It's my definition of success! It truly makes up for some of the tougher times I've had during this obsessive journey.

SCREAM QUEEN COLLECTION, VOL. 1
REVIEWED BY MIKE HAUSHALTER

I have been watching a lot of fun streaming stuff on Tubi lately. Not too long ago, I checked out one of the many, many *Witchcraft* sequels, *Witchcraft X: Mistress of the Craft* to be exact. I noticed one of its more prominent stars is SOV Scream Queen Stephanie Beaton, an actress I instantly remembered from back in the day (I even interviewed her at one point), but who fell off my radar for many a year. After a quick look at her body of work (which includes three *Witchcraft* outings) on IMDb, I thought it was time to dig back into her oeuvre. I decided to begin my journey with a three-DVD box set that Beaton's own company, Silver Moon Productions, put out: *Scream Queen Collection, Vol. 1*. The set contains *Eyes of the Werewolf*, *The Bagman*, and *Evil in the Bayou*, all of which feature Beaton, and the last of which happens to be the film she was about to make when I interviewed her way back when.

Eyes of the Werewolf (1999)
After chemist Rich Stevens (Mark Sawyer) is blinded in a horrible laboratory accident, he receives an experimental emergency eye transplant from the unethical Dr. Atwill (Tim Sullivan, also half of the film's directorial team). While the procedure is successful, the gang of redneck thugs that Atwill utilizes to acquire body parts for his experimental transplant surgeries unknowingly supplies him with the eyes of a werewolf. When the moon is full, Rich changes into a beast and begins to take bloody revenge on anyone who has wronged him.

Eyes of the Werewolf is a low-rent, SOV creature-feature from writer/director Sullivan (*The Laughing Dead*) and codirector Jeff Leroy (*Werewolf in a Women's Prison*) that has a lot to offer werewolf and exploitation fans alike. For werewolf fans, there's the big, hulking, snarling werewolf; Androse, a mystical dwarf who helps guide the hero on his journey; plenty of Wolfman Easter eggs; and the intriguing idea of the transmission of

lycanthropy through organ transplant. For the exploitation fan, the film offers tons of blood and gore. Beaton is a tough lesbian police detective who is featured prominently in two loves scenes.

This is not to say the film doesn't have its downsides. That werewolf I mentioned? Well, its costume is way cooler-looking than it is scary or convincing. The film looks cruddy, even by shot-on-video standards, and the day-for-night photography is on par with Ed Wood's *The Bride of the Beast*. The film also doesn't have the greatest of casts.

At the end of the day, all pros and cons aside, if you're a fan of SOV films, you're probably going to enjoy *Eyes of the Werewolf*, but if you're not, I doubt this will be the film to change your mind.

The Bagman (2002)

To paraphrase Silver Moon Productions: Fifteen years ago, Jack Marshall lost both his parents and was horribly disfigured in a mysterious house fire. After five years of Jack being mercilessly teased by his peers, his private hell came to an end when he was beaten and drowned by one of his classmates. Years later, Sue Creswell (Beaton) returns to her hometown for a class reunion. The terror begins as, one by one, her old classmates begin to disappear. Meanwhile, an unknown, silent caller torments Sue, leading her to wonder if Jack Marshall is really dead.

Despite having a title that brings to mind an organized crime thriller, *The Bagman* is actually an old-school stalk-and-slay revenge story in the vein of *Slaughter High* or *I Know What You Did Last Summer*.

The Bagman is a rough-around-the-edges low-budget-horror effort that covers all the bases. It has a decent storyline, with a few last-minute twists, and while the killer's identity is never in question, some of his motives are. There is a bit of skin on display courtesy of Beaton (who also produced the film) during a hot stovetop sex scene. The film also has a very decent body count (seven or eight, depending on your count). Gory highlights include some dismemberments, a trip through a meat grinder, some stabbings, a very brutal eye-gouging, and a wicked head-cleaving with a machete. Heads up to any dog lover out there who may check out this film: There is a doggy death.

Some downsides to the film include uninspired camera work, poor lighting, and listless dialogue. The cast is a little squeaky here and there—no worse than other films of this ilk, but not much better either. The editing is also rough at times.

Minus its lack of flashy film stock and big-name starlets, *The Bagman* is nearly on par with the Hollywood horror efforts of its day, though it goes the extra mile of showing some skin and some very messy, bloody deaths.

Evil in the Bayou (2003)

Evil in the Bayou is a low-budget, SOV, cops-versus-Satanists horror mystery written by, directed by, and starring Beaton. In the film, ex-cop-turned-PI Jake Le'Claire (Paul Zanone) searches for the missing wife of a client named Ryan Mason. When he finds the body of his client's wife rotting in the bayou, the sleuth is led into a deadly world of voodoo, human sacrifices, and evil Satanists.

As I spend more and more time on this Earth, I find it harder to relate to films in which evil Satanists are trying to unleash Satan himself to take over the world. For one thing, real-life Satanists are in the news all the time these days for the good things they are trying to accomplish, such as fighting racism and homophobia and protecting abortion rights—usually at the expense of one of the so-called "good" religious organizations. So, now, when I read or hear about Satan being blamed for a real-world problem, I just instantly cry, "Bullshit!" I have to admit, I feel pretty much the same when it's brought up in a film, as it is here. In addition, I found it quaint that the evil Satanists presented in *Evil in the Bayou* are very much of the old '60s- and '70s-era variety: mostly just thinly veiled stand-ins for hippies and other folks who did not conform to middle-American morals. The Satanists in the film also seemed very at odds with the voodoo angle presented in the film's opening text crawl, which made me a bit leery of the journey I was about to take.

It turns out that by the time the end credits rolled, I was pleasantly surprised with where the story went. A lot of my problems with the opening half of the film were explained away in rather clever ways, and it all played out pretty well by the end of the picture.

To be sure, *Evil in the Bayou* is a very threadbare-looking movie with an awful lot of tarps and Spirit Halloween props. But all in all, I was pretty entertained by the film. It has an earnest cast, including stand-outs Zanone (*The Bagman*), Randal Malone (*Dahmer vs. Gacy*), and Beaton, who gives a fine performance. It also has a decent script and a fair amount of bloodletting. As Beaton's first full-length feature as director, *Evil in the Bayou* is a decent middle-of-the-road outing and the highlight of the films in its box set.

NON-OBJECTIVE REVIEWS

Bette Cassatt as Narcissa Sentinel in *A Sweet and Vicious Beauty* (Photo courtesy Eric Thornett.)

You know the drill by now: We either know the filmmakers or, in at least one of the following cases, were involved with the production. That doesn't mean we shouldn't talk about these projects! Either way, here are some cool things you might have missed.

A Sweet and Vicious Beauty (2012, Piranha Pictures)

"In the town of Harbor Bridge, it is said that when someone dies, his last breath stays in his throat. When the head is severed, that last breath can be taken by another, and the recipient becomes stronger. Narcissa Sentinel (Bette Cassatt) has been robbing graves to cure her illness with these last breaths...but soon realizes that perhaps fresher specimens are in order. Shot locally, A Sweet and Vicious Beauty is an epic Gothic Victorian movie that shows the journey of Sentinel from a sickly woman to a bloodthirsty mass murderer who terrorizes the town. From spooky old houses to headless zombies, *this film has it all!"*[1]

Director Eric Thornett has been responsible for some of my favorite movies, particularly the weird noir *Shockheaded*. (The usual disclosure: Amy Lynn Best and I have very brief cameos in, and shot second unit for, Thornett's *Fifth City*.) *A Sweet and Vicious Beauty* is his best movie yet. It's gorgeous, for one thing, evoking Corman's Poe films, and I don't say that lightly.

At the heart is a pair of terrific performances by Sara Cole and, especially, Bette Cassatt. (Second disclosure: This movie is why Amy cast Bette in our film *Razor Days*.) The roles in *A Sweet and Vicious Beauty* are demanding, and the performances are nuanced. And again, there are headless ghosts. (Me: "How can they see where they're going?" Eric: "They're *ghosts*!")

Best of all, the film is available both on Blu-ray (through Gold Ninja Video, at Goldninjavideo.com) and streaming, via Amazon Prime.

Skinned Deep (2004, Center Ring Entertainment)

Back in *ExNat* #8, we talked to director and effects master Gabe Bartalos and told you all about *Skinned Deep*, Bartalos's ode to the insane backwoods family, with the dial turned way the fuck past 11. Warwick Davis (*Leprechaun*) and Jay Dugre (*Saint Bernard*) star as Plates and Brain, respectively, two of the more reasonable members of the twisted clan.

Severin Films recently gave *Skinned Deep* the royal treatment, and it looks and sounds better than ever. The Blu-ray is chock-full of extras, including a nifty bonus of Gabe, COVID-bound in his studio, reading interview questions only a little like a serial killer would.

Grab this one, and Gabe's mind-melting follow-up, *Saint Bernard*, at Severinfilms.com.

Tales of Poe (2012, Mastropieces; Southpaw Pictures)

Yep, there's no way I can talk about *Tales of Poe* objectively. Amy Lynn Best and I were associate producers on this one. We're also both in the second segment, "The Cask," based on Poe's *The Cask of Amontillado* and costarring Randy Jones (aka the cowboy from the Village People), and man, was that a fun weekend shoot.

Directors Alan Rowe Kelly and Bart Mastronardi came aboard our film

---

[1] Thornett, Eric, and C.W. Prather. "Plot Summary." *IMDb*, IMDb.com, Inc., www.imdb.com/title/tt2438658/plotsummary.

Razor Days in the midst of shooting the following three reimaginings of Poe's works: "The Tell-Tale Heart," starring Kelly, Debbie Rochon, Desiree Gould (*Sleepaway Camp*), and Lesleh Donaldson (*Curtains*); the aforementioned "The Cask," starring and directed by Kelly, with Jones, Best, Brewster McCall, Susan Adriensen, Jerry Murdock, and Zoe Chlandla; and the epic poem "Dreams" (adapted by Michael Varrati and Mastronardi, the latter of whom also directed), a phantasmagoria of imagery starring Bette Cassatt[2], Adrienne King (*Friday the 13th*), Caroline Williams (*Texas Chainsaw Massacre 2*), Amy Steel (*Friday the 13th Part 2*), and dancer Cartier Williams.

Bart Mastronardi is a brilliant cinematographer, and *Tales of Poe* is a hands down gorgeous film. I'd say that regardless. The project was also a long road to hoe for both Bart and Alan, so it's with no little excitement that I tell you *Tales of Poe* is available streaming and for digital download. Check out this wonder that plays with the themes of classic literature and brings Poe's works to new life (and, in the case of his poem "Dreams," to film for the first time ever!).

---

2 Indie filmmakers are incestuous. Amidst these productions, we traded roles like square dancers.

"Saturn's Core Audio & Video is a New Jersey based home video label devoted to releasing underground oddities and shot on video cinema on VHS, and now, blu-ray discs! In partnership with OCN Distribution, Saturn's Core will exhume forgotten or under-seen genre cinema from the 80s and 90s, with an emphasis on SOV horror features. Vinegar Syndrome's sister company, OCN Distribution, is thrilled to be representing this diverse and unique home video line!"

— Vinegar Syndrome official website[1]

I was tempted to reiterate the usual disclaimer here: "We know these cats, and we know the folks whose movies they're putting out, yadda yadda yadda." But you knew that already.

As I've already pointed out, Saturn's Core's Ross Snyder and Bill Hellfire are doing Cinemagogue's work in bringing back some true classics of indie horror. It's difficult to explain just how foundational these movies are, both in terms of film history and their impact on fellow (and future) indie filmmakers.

Wherever you set the "beginning" of indie filmmaking—with the Transgressives, the Warhol experiments, or Tim Ritter's *Truth or Dare?*, finding mainstream success in the early days of the mom-and-pops, "like a circle in a spiral, like a wheel within a wheel"—outsider

---
1 "Details." *Vinegar Syndrome*, https://vinegarsyndrome.com/products/savage-harvest-saturns-core.

and underground filmmakers were responding to a call within themselves that was being fed, consciously or un-, by a movement. "Art for art's sake" was the thesis, "Fuck the studios" the corollary, and "Let's make the movies the way we want to make them" the goal.

Snyder and Hellfire have been diving into the deep end of the shot-on-video historical pool and uncovering some true marvels. Now, your enjoyment of these movies will vary with your tolerance for technical difficulties. Resist being a snob. Remember, Truffaut and Goddard were working out their own rules while contributing to *Cahiers du Cinéma*, so none of your complaints will be anything new.

In addition, the stories behind the making of these movies are often just as entertaining as the finished films. *Red Spirit Lake/We Await* (1993/1996): Charles Pinion's double feature has the handsomest packaging, true,

and a remarkable liner booklet that is, in many ways, the Rosetta Stone of indie filmmaking and punk rock. Both films begin with punches to the head, literally and figuratively, and the violence is visceral. But Pinion's narratives are built on visuals that amount to a mountain of shifting sand. The wrong herbal accompaniment to *We Await* could be traumatic, but that's the only trigger warning you're getting here. Also, whether you're a filmmaker or just a student of film history, *do not* skip the commentaries, nor should you take lightly the scene deconstructions in the bonus sections.

Savage Harvest (1994): *"St. Louis, Missouri based writer/director Eric Stanze (*The Scare Game, Scrapbook, Ratline*) made major waves in the underground with this ambitious, Native American themed,* Evil Dead-*style demonic possession romp filmed against the backdrop of the Great Flood of 1993; a real life debilatating disaster that devastated parts of the American Midwest. Elaborate practical effects, extreme chainsaw violence, a memorable monster, and some genuine atmospheric scares helped put* Savage Harvest *on the map and cemented Stanze's status as one of the most consistent and visionary auteurs working in the shot on video horror medium."*[2]

So entereth Wicked Pixel Cinema and Eric Stanze. Stanze is another guy whose roots in experimental film are all over his work. Following Stanze's debut film, *The Scare Game* (which was, if I recall, the basis for his trippy *Ice from the Sun*), *Savage Harvest* predates his down-to-earth-and-fucking-terrifying serial killer/abduction story, *Scrapbook*. In the *Savage Harvest* special features, Stanze admits that he was initially disappointed with the final version of *Harvest* because it never lived up to the balls-to-the-wall, *Evil Dead*-esque nightmare living inside his head. Well, if *Savage Harvest* is a disappointment, it's no wonder Stanze's successes are so amazing (*Deadwood Park*, I'm looking at you).

Even as an early offering, *Savage Harvest* ticks a lot of the Stanze boxes: graphic violence, including at least one bit that will churn your stomach; a long, complicated backstory for the upcoming bloodshed that is nonetheless enthralling; surprisingly good performances from obviously first-time actors; a dizzying visual style that never slows down once the pace slips into its highest gear; and a feeling of both dread and exhilaration at the end.

Don't skip the rerelease's new documentary, "A Quarter Century Since the Harvest," which begins almost as heartbreakingly as *Lost in La Mancha*, as Stanze, Ross, and many others set up at a drive-in just as a massive storm rolls through. You get to watch the indie, punk rock filmmaker spirit in action here, and it's inspiring.

Sinistre (1995): *"The feature debut from Springfield, Missouri based video director Ronnie Sortor (*Ravage*), * Sinistre *is an awe-inspiring, post-Tarantino, heist/haunted house mash up that instantly marked the emergence of a fresh and unique voice withing the '90s SOV scene. A mix of manic action*

---

2 Ibid.

set pieces, nightmarish surrealism, and entrail ripping, head stomping gore courtesy of FX artist Mike Strain (You're Next, V/H/S) Saturn's Core is proud to present Sinistre *in its first and definitive Blu-Ray edition, fully approved and supervised by director Ronnie Sortor."*[3]

Sinistre (sometimes spelled Sinyster) is another gut-punch being rereleased by Saturn's Core. While Pinion sneaks some humor into his horror, Ronnie Sortor keeps Sinistre mean and nasty to the end. Utilizing one of my personal favorite story lines (Mean and nasty criminals hole up in a place filled with things even meaner and nastier), Sinistre features crooks who find themselves up against an axe-wielding phantasm and his minions, which means torture and horror is very much on the menu.

Sinistre was on my original slate of movies to promote back when I worked for Ron Bonk's Sub Rosa Studios Cinema. Unfortunately, both the VHS and DVD were muddy, ugly transfers, so this new Blu-ray

---

[3] "Details." *Vinegar Syndrome*, https://vinegarsyndrome.com/products/sinistre-saturns-core.

is a miracle. Sortor supervised two different versions of the film, and he walks the viewer through every agonizing step.

Shatter Dead (1994): If you're a regular reader of *Exploitation Nation*, you know the name Scooter McCrae. An early and important name in indie horror, McCrae made a name for himself with this tragic, existential zombie movie, in no small part thanks to the film's tagline: "God Hates You."

In *Shatter Dead*, Susan (Stark Raven) is just trying to get back home to her boyfriend, navigating streets where the undead beg for food and money. Thanks to an angelic rape, the dead just don't die anymore. They don't want brains, and they don't shuffle around. They're just sad, second-class citizens. And they're getting sick of that kind of treatment. Meanwhile, the usual (or unusual) religious assholes are using the phenomena for their own purposes.

Unflinching in its violence (and nudity—the infamous gun-fuck scene has never been cleaner), *Shatter Dead* is sick, sad, tragic, nihilistic, and hilarious. I can't recommend this film enough.

Well, OK, I can and will, because….

Yes! Happy Cloud Publishing is proud to release *The Shatter Dead Companion*, a unique look at the titular indie classic, written by the film's director, Scooter McCrae.

The Shatter Dead Companion includes McCrae's original screenplay, annotated by the screenwriter. This is accompanied by rare (and a few never-before-scene) production stills, promotional stills, cover art, and magazine reproductions. It even recounts the time *Shatter Dead* was decried on the floor of Parliament during the Video Nasties hysteria.

If that weren't enough, *The Shatter Dead Companion* also includes never-before-seen treatments for proposed sequels, as well as the official full-length, as-yet-unproduced-but-there-is-still-time-we-are-still-young-god-damn-it sequel.

All of this comes in a handsome, full-color, thick-as-a-door-stop edition, handsomely introduced by Michael Gingold. It would look great on a coffee table or side table…any table, really—just don't set your drink on it; we worked hard on this thing.

Available now at www.happycloudpublishing.com or at Amazons near you.

Indonesian Horror

by Jason Lane

There has been a marked surge in both the number and quality of horror films coming from Indonesia, to the point where I began to wonder, why the sudden increase? And why hasn't there been a decent representation before now, not just in horror, but in any regard? In terms of history, Indonesian cinema is fascinating in that it started later than the cinema of other cultures but established itself as equal to the rest of the world in a relatively short time.

A small history: The Republic of Indonesia is a country located off the southern coast of mainland Asia. It is situated between the Indian and Pacific oceans and consists of roughly 17,000 islands, among which are Java, Sumatra, and parts of New Guinea and Borneo. It is the world's largest island country and the fourteenth largest country by area. More than 270 million people live in Indonesia, with Java housing half the country's population. So, how has a place so big, with this many people, not put more of a stamp on pop culture? There are a few reasons.

- Between 1926 and 1965, little film production took place. Although the Indonesian film industry is now the fastest-growing subsector of the country's creative economy, producing and promoting films

just weren't of high importance to the populace. Between '65 and '98, heavy censorship under the rule of President Suharto enforced the idea that Indonesian cinema should only show/produce/make films that were educational or culture-positive. In the late '60s and the '70s, this censorship loosened slightly, leading to the production of several erotic films (!), which the government loved so much that in '72, it cracked down hard on the industry, especially concerning sexual content. The '80s saw a revival of the industry, but not by much. Most of the movies made during that time were quick, cheap copycats of blockbuster movies. The '90s were a low point, as imports of foreign films revived and TV had a higher impact than before. An example? In '90, Indonesians made just 115 films. In '93, they made 37. In '96, they made 33. In '99, they made seven.

- There were governmental issues. Indonesia usually attached a high tax to foreign films, so seeing things from other parts of the world was difficult. However, Suharto's overthrowal in '98 brought greater freedoms to the country, with freedom of speech being a prevalent one. Filmmakers were finally allowed to be more honest and daring in their subject matter, and we're reaping the benefits as an audience now.

- Indonesia has the largest population of Muslims of any country. While I'm not stating this as a fact, I can speculate as to why Indonesians haven't had a bigger impact on cinema: Some Muslims consider cinema *haram*, or something sinful that the Quran and the Sunnah have prohibited. While only a small percentage of Muslims think of cinema as a punishable transgression, there is a consensus, especially during those times mentioned, that films are considered forbidden and a waste of time.

Indonesian cinema has had a truly rocky history. In addition, I've noticed that it has been a kind of mystery in the horror community. Up until just a few years ago, I heard very few people talk about the quality of films from that part of the world.

The best avenue for foreign horror lately has been the Shudder app, and if you are truly a fan of horror, get this app. Indonesian cinema is shown prominently there, and thankfully so.

The following are some films of note.

- **Beranak Dalam Kubur/Birth in the Grave (1971)**: This is a very slow burn, but its seen-it-before ending makes for a great payoff (Seeing someone get knocked out in a fight doesn't make you want to skip seeing other people getting knocked out, right?). Disturbing settings, gooey makeup, and fairly decent acting boost the cliché story of a bad sister trying to doom the good sister by any means to get the family fortune. Insert curses and the undead in place of blackmail and murder. The film was remade in 2007, but the remake is awful.

- **Ratu Ilmu Hitam/The Queen of Black Magic (1979)**: Plenty of over-the-top, gory moments really drive home the gonzo-filmmaking feel of this movie. Bee attacks, flying heads, exploding veins, a self-decapitation, and an exploding body are just the tip of the iceberg in this movie about a woman who, after being wrongly accused of witchcraft and thrown off a cliff by angry townspeople, survives and learns witchcraft to exact revenge (You kind of had to see that coming). There is also a very well-made remake of this film that came out in 2019 (and is discussed later in this article).

- **Leák/Mystics in Bali (1981)**: While not great, this movie is still a landmark in Indonesian horror and one of the first cult classics to really get noticed by horror fans in the States. Of note is that the story deals with a Leák, a flying, disembodied head with its body's internal organs still dangling from its neck. Curses, weird camera angles, plenty of gore, and the aforementioned flying head make this a wild ride that needs to be seen to be appreciated.

- **Rumah Dara/Dara/Macabre (2009)**: The first full-length horror film by the Mo Brothers is a doozy, doubling as a psychological thriller while delving heavily into the well-mined trope of the cannibalistic, batshit, psycho family. There are two things you can do with a cliché in cinema: One option is to come up with an original take on the established cliché, and the other option is if you can't add to it, outdo it. The Mo Brothers find themselves meeting the challenge easily with buckets of blood, unapologetic

violence, and damn near comedy in some scenes (Take note of the POV shots of the chainsaws). Think of this movie as a more beautifully shot, less funny, more vicious *House of 1,000 Corpses*.

- **"Safe Haven," *V/H/S/2* (2013)**: This is probably most people's introduction to Indonesian horror. It's also kind of a cheat because it's one of the short-film segments comprising the *VHS* anthology series, but damn if this isn't worthy of a mention. "Safe Haven" concerns a documentary crew filming a Jim Jones-style cult that foreshadows a worse-than-imaginable apocalypse. Do the high-speed shots, rising tension, and imaginative cuts seem familiar to you? The film was directed by Timo Tjahjanto, one half of the Mo Brothers, and Gareth Evans, who directed Indonesian action vehicles *The Raid* and *The Raid 2*.

- ***Pengabdi Setan/Satan's Slaves* (2017)**: This movie has everything you could ask for: mounting dread, terror, limited jump scares, and a rich, developed plot that ties everything together. I really wish I could see this film on the big screen rather than on my television, because it's one of those movies that you really need to take everything in to appreciate it. The film is directed by Joko Anwar (Remember this guy's name—you're going to see it a lot in quality Indonesian filmmaking).

- ***Sebelum Iblis Menjemput/May the Devil Take You* (2018)**: Another film by Timo Tjahjanto, this one is solid as hell, featuring generic scenes done with fresh eyes. It's a very *Evil Dead*-inspired type of movie, one in which a girl finds out about her family's abandoned, creepy house (that they never mentioned before) and needs to go investigate it. Think that's a good idea? It is for the viewers, as while the film isn't perfect, it's still fun as hell. And it leads right into the sequel….

- ***Sebelum Iblis Menjemput: Ayat Dua/May the Devil Take You Too* (2020)**: Timo Tjahjanto returns to direct this sequel. I don't want to give any spoilers away by even mentioning characters or survivors from the first film here, so I'll just say that while this film is not quite as good as the first one, it's still damn good.

- ***Perempuan Tanah Jahanam/ Impetigore* (2019)**: *Perempuan Tanah Jahanam* was selected to represent Indonesia as a nominee for Best International Feature Film at the 2121 Academy Awards. When a horror film gets a nod over other genres, that tells you something. It's directed by Joko Anwar (the director of the aforementioned *Pengabdi Setan* [aka *Satan's Slaves*]), in collaboration with the people who produced *The Wailing*. With that pedigree alone, it should be good, and it is. It was nominated for over 29 awards at various film festivals and won nine of them, and these were categories like Best Picture, Best Director, and Best Supporting Actor/Actress. Anwar brings his eye for detail and skin-crawling terror to this movie about a woman who travels with a friend to a remote village to solve a mystery and finds sheer hell on earth. The subject matter reminds one of *The Exorcist* in that the subject is unnerving and the last 30 minutes get gonzo awesome.

- ***Ratu Ilmu Hitam/The Queen of Black Magic* (2019)**: This is the loose remake of the 1981 Indonesian horror film mentioned earlier, though it's much more serious in tone. Synopsis: Three young men take their spouses to the creepy orphanage where they were raised to meet the creepy old guy who raised them. Spoiler: There's something creepy AF going on at the orphanage. Whereas the original was an over-the-top splatterfest, this one is much more disturbing and, dare I say, creepy.

A short note about the Cinema of Transgression

In a serendipitous turn of events, founding members of the Cinema of Transgression have popped up all over this issue, so I thought it best to take a moment to talk about what the heck we've been talking about.

"Cinema of Transgression" was a term coined by filmmaker Nick Zedd (*Geek Maggot Bingo*) back in 1985 to describe "a New York City-based underground film movement, consisting of a loose-knit group of like-minded artists using shock value and black humor in their films."[1] Notables in this movement included Zedd, Jon Moritsugu, Kembra Pfahler, David Wojnarowicz, Tessa Hughes-Freeland, Richard Kern, Beth B, Casandra Stark, Tommy Turner, Lydia Lunch, and Manuel DeLanda, all of whom, between the late '70s and mid-'80s, made cheap, weird, violent, semi- and straight-up pornographic, low-budget, 8mm and Super 8mm movies. Think Stan Brakhage at hardcore punk shows. Maybe not.

The Kern collections, *Hardcore, Volumes 1 & 2* (put out by *Film Threat* back in the day), introduced many of us to the Cinema of Transgression. In my case, we passed these uncomfortable, unsettling bits of weird-ass punk spirit around at Pittsburgh Filmmakers.

In the '80s, Zedd[2] published a zine called *The Underground Film Bulletin*, running reviews and interviews with Lower East Side filmmakers as a promotional tool for his own stuff. In his famous fourth issue, which included articles on Stark, DeLanda, and Jim Jarmusch, Zedd (publishing under the name Orion Jeriko) included the "Cinema of Transgression Manifesto." Thus, the movement was born.

The manifesto is reprinted in its entirety on the following pages (with permission from nobody).

---

1 "Cinema of Transgression." *Wikipedia*, Wikimedia Foundation, Inc., https://en.wikipedia.org/wiki/Cinema_of_Transgression. (I'm busy, *okay*?)

2 *ExNat* readers may recall Zedd had a relationship with Reverend Jen Miller, who appeared in these very pages in Issue #7. Zedd passed away on February 27, 2022.

The Cinema of Transgression Manifesto

We who have violated the laws, commands and duties of the avant-garde; i.e. to bore, tranquilize and obfuscate through a fluke process dictated by practical convenience stand guilty as charged. We openly renounce and reject the entrenched academic snobbery which erected a monument to laziness known as structuralism and proceeded to lock out those filmmakers who posessed the vision to see through this charade.

We refuse to take their easy approach to cinematic creativity; an approach which ruined the underground of the sixties when the scourge of the film school took over. Legitimising every mindless manifestation of sloppy movie making undertaken by a generation of misled film students, the dreary media arts centres and geriatic cinema critics have totally ignored the exhilarating accomplishments of those in our rank—such underground invisibles as Zedd, Kern, Turner, Klemann, DeLanda, Eros and Mare, and DirectArt Ltd, a new generation of filmmakers daring to rip out of the stifling straight jackets of film theory in a direct attack on every value system known to man.

We propose that all film schools be blown up and all boring films never be made again. We propose that a sense of humour is an essential element discarded by the doddering academics and further, that any film which doesn't shock isn't worth looking at. All values must be challenged. Nothing is sacred. Everything must be questioned and reassessed in order to free our minds from the faith of tradition. Intellectual growth demands that risks be taken and changes occur in political, sexual and aesthetic alignments no matter who disapproves. We propose to go beyond all limits set or prescribed by taste, morality or any other traditional value system shackling the minds of men. We pass beyond and go over boundaries of millimeters, screens and projectors to a state of expanded cinema.

We violate the command and

law that we bore audiences to death in rituals of circumlocution and propose to break all the taboos of our age by sinning as much as possible. There will be blood, shame, pain and ecstasy, the likes of which no one has yet imagined. None shall emerge unscathed. Since there is no afterlife, the only hell is the hell of praying, obeying laws, and debasing yourself before authority figures, the only heaven is the heaven of sin, being rebellious, having fun, fucking, learning new things and breaking as many rules as you can. This act of courage is known as transgression. We propose transformation through transgression—to convert, transfigure and transmute into a higher plane of existence in order to approach freedom in a world full of unknowing slaves.[1]

---

[1] Zedd, Nick. "Cinema of Transgression Manifesto." *The Underground Film Bulletin*, no. 4, Sept. 1985.

TRUST THE WITCH: LYDIA LUNCH AND RETROVIRUS

CONCERT AND DVD REVIEW BY DR. RHONDA BAUGHMAN

Lydia Lunch.

Lydia *fucking* Lunch.

Her name evokes an adrenaline rush, a few wicked downlow tickles, and the immediate desire to angrily *create something*. It doesn't surprise me that Lunch remains underground, off major labels, and anti-commercial. Not for the easily offended, her résumé screams a tornado of collaborations, photography, appearances, performance art, writing, music, theatre, spoken word, workshops, film, and video (and probably more artistic mediums I'm unaware of). There's something *epic* about the fact her creative output numbers in the hundreds—possibly thousands—and there's still not only works of hers for me to discover, but Lydia Lunch is still *not* a household name. Yet she's not exactly a secret either. She's also definitely on my list of top influential artists of *both* the 20th and the 21st centuries.

Lunch arrived on the New York City punk landscape at age 16 and roared through the city in the late '70s, leaving her first mark on the no-wave scene with her noisy, brief, but highly influential band Teenage Jesus and the Jerks. This was followed over the years by major multimedia collaborations with Nick Zedd, Richard Kern, Exene Cervenka, J.G. Thirlwell, and Sonic Youth, just to name a few. Now in her early 60s, Lunch remains a force to be reckoned with onstage, performing with the bands Big Sexy Noise and Retrovirus, while her podcast, *The Lydian Spin*, continues to be a major highlight amid pandemic madness.

Buzzbin, Canton, Ohio: September 9, 2021

I'm not sure many Canton, Ohio, residents knew we were graced by punk rock royalty on September 9, 2021. It still surprises *me*, and I was there. A total dream come true, this show was important not just because it was my first since the pandemic hit hard (for me, November 2019, with the official lockdown beginning March 24, 2020), but because Lunch performs mostly overseas or in big U.S. cities nowhere near me. So, Lydia Lunch came to doinky football metropolis Canton, Ohio. I still think about it from time to time, especially when I drive past the venue she performed in and the rancid Ohio air whispers, "Yes, Rhonda. She was really here."

Lunch and Retrovirus were on the bill for FemmeFest, the brainchild of Julia Jezmund Bentley, who, along with her husband, owns the venue Buzzbin. Three-day passes were only $25. It was a smashing lineup, I'll admit. The list of bands (all of which have FB or Bandcamp pages for further info) for the three-day event included: Kearstin Clark, Samantha Morrow, Buick Audra, The Super Babes, The Long Hunt, Electro Cult Circus, The Ex-Bombers, Spider Lilies, Dump Cake, Wearebaby, Rodeo Boys, Garter Shake, Night Goat, Athena Rex, Escuela Grind, and Mr. Clit and the Pink Cigarettes.

FemmeFest was quietly advertised, and thank god for the randomness of the Instagram algorithm. It's the only reason I even noticed Lydia Lunch Retrovirus was coming.

So, I was going to get to see Lunch, finally, as I have wanted to do for 20 years, but I was also going to get Weasel Walter (guitar), Tim Dahl (bass), and Bob Bert (drums). Three more fucking legends were coming to town! It was my Christmas in September. It was better than Christmas: I didn't have to diddle through Godly carols; instead, I heard the voices and musical arrangements of a few rock gods.

Before Retrovirus took the stage, I enjoyed the music, fashion, and stage presence of the opener, Indianapolis-based Mr. Clit and the Pink Cigarettes, even going so far as to snag a masked pic with bassist Abby Hart; I figured since they're from Indianapolis, and my heart was left in Indianapolis,

Lydia Lunch at Chateau H, France, April 2019 (Photo by Sébastien Greppo. All Rights Reserved.)

the selfie would make me feel a bit better (It did). I stayed for a few songs from Escuela Grind, also digging their vitality onstage. However, I forgot earplugs[1] and so had to take my ass outside and listen from a distance.

Lydia Lunch will be in downtown Canton. I had no clue what that would entail, but it was all I needed to hear to get me out of the house and ready to stampede through crowds where, as I suspected, about one in five wore a mask. My concert-comrade in crime had to check out early, but I stuck it out to the 11:15 p.m. headliner start time and the 12:15 a.m. merch stand hit.[2] It was too late for an interview—everyone was tired. Also, there were way too many unmasked people milling about, and for some reason, super loud music coming from overhead, so I had to shout through my mask. Lunch did confirm most of the songs I heard live were on those two CDs I bought: *Urge to Kill*, by Lunch/Retrovirus, and the music companion to the Beth B film *The War Is Never Over*. I highly recommend both.

In an interview with *Forte*, Lunch had said: *"Right now, considering the global disasters we're all facing on so many levels, I think it's time to just fucking ROCK! Truly, truly. On so many

Dr. Rhonda with Abby from Mr. Clit and the Pink Cigarettes

fronts, we're really in a contagious period right now, so obviously with a name like Retrovirus, I mean I wish our disease was the cure…we have to rebel somehow, so we will rebel with rock!"*[3] She takes her role as HGA[4] seriously. As soon as Lunch took the stage, dressed in black, signature red lipstick, hot as hell, and full of sass, she dubbed Canton "Cunton" and had some hecklers in the audience who thought they had something interesting to shout (They did not) shushing the fuck up and staring into their beers. I would have fallen in love right there if I weren't already enamored of her entire career.

"Snakepit Breakdown" started

---

[1] I usually carry them with me, but since the pandemic, I've not seen a concert since November 2019. I'll not forget again.

[2] I have finally learned my lesson: If you see the merch and you love the merch, buy the fucking merch. Just throw down the cash, because chances are, it's tour-exclusive. Ironically, my irritating inner other, often also a hyper-fiscally responsible adult, balked at the "Trust the Witch" tee and tote. And I DO trust the witch, so I'm hoping some asshole pops them up on eBay.

[3] Abbott, Renée N. "Lydia Lunch Returns to Australia with Retrovirus." *Forte*, Furst Media, https://fortemag.com.au/lydia-lunch-returns-to-australia-with-retrovirus/.

[4] For some, "HGA" refers to the witchy term *holy guardian angel* (I also refer to it as *harsh gospel ambassador*). Lunch has been creatively producing her truth for over 40 years; some may just not like to hear all she has to say. And why would they? Lunch has even less patience for bullshit than I do.

us off, and from then on, the night belonged to Lunch and Retrovirus. Songs rolled in waves: "Dead Me You Beside," "Love Split with Blood," "The Gospel Singer," and "Tied and Twist," to name a few, but it was that last song, "Forever on the Run," that hung in the air like sweat mixed with a heavy perfume, the kind of scent that you believe still clings to a dead lover's shirt, so you keep it around long after they're gone. "Something witchy in the air tonight." It felt like the lyric went on forever—"Something witchy in the air tonight"—and indeed, in my mind, the phrase remains weeks later, as it should. The words felt ritualistic, like a chant, like a war cry. "Something witchy in the air tonight." It was the perfect aurally magical end to an imperfectly violent small-town night. Besides, there's *always* something witchy in the air if you're smart enough to notice and attune to its wavelength.

Lydia Lunch (Photo by Dr. Rhonda Baughman.)

DVD Review: *The War Is Never Over*
What a 78-minute masterpiece from Beth B!

The War Is Never Over (2019) was an official selection at three 2020 film festivals: SXSW, International Film Festival Rotterdam, and DOC NYC.

My only complaint is that the film is too short, but then again, I feel this way about most of Lunch's work—her entire body of work, which I've consumed over the years like a greedy addict who needs one more minute, one more song, one more show—but I know it's not just me anymore. She has fans all over the world. All hail Queen Lydia! Her voice reaches some people when nothing else can—and for over 40 years now—writhing and shouting and stalking and addressing, bleeding and preaching and performing and undressing—and all in the name of owning her own body, her own mind, her own space, her own life. Apologizing to no one (for no apologies ever need be made), she knows us all better than we can fake it. Most people don't really want to climb to the top floor, can't dangle from the edge; far below waits the plaza of truth, and the fall is far. Better to linger by the rooftop pool, dip toes in the murky immortal waters of the American Dream, watch the sun and horizon wage war. Wars will continue around you whether you join in the fray or not, whether you pick up a weapon and fire or not; death will come for you whether you want to think about it or not. War and death are timeless. They're never over. They have all the time in the world and—seated next to you right now, breathing on you, clouding your peripheral vision—they'll wait.

by Mike Haushalter

One of my favorite activities is to look through bargain bins and the racks of secondhand sellers to find movie deals. Whether it's a forgotten A-list title, a blink-and-you-missed-it indie release, or last year's hot direct-to-home-video title, as long as it costs $2 to $5, it's bound to come home with me. If it's less than that? Well, I'm willing to take a gamble on almost anything that's priced at a dollar and hints even a tiny bit of intrigue or interest. After all, I can't even rent most of these things for that price, and if they don't work out, I can sell them again. But when they do work out, it's magical. Here's the roundup of my latest finds, good and bad.

Zoolander (2001)

The box says: "Clear the runway for Derek Zoolander (Ben Stiller), VH1's three-time male model of the year. His face falls when hippie-chic Hansel (Owen Wilson) scooters in to steal this year's award. The evil fashion guru Mugatu (Will Ferrell) seizes the opportunity to turn Derek into a killing machine. It's a well-designed conspiracy, and only with the help of Hansel and a few well-chosen accessories, like Matilda (Christine Taylor), can Derek make the world safe for male models everywhere."

Why I risked a dollar: Well, I had never seen it before. That's pretty much it. I had recently seen some clips from *Zoolander* on YouTube that

really made me think I should give the film a look, and for a dollar, it couldn't be passed up.

Thoughts: Other than the fact that I hate Ben Stiller, I am not sure why it took more than 20 years for me to check out *Zoolander*. But here we are, and what a deliriously fun comedy it was. I was super impressed with the film and how good Stiller was in it, as much as it pains me to say that. It's no *Tropic Thunder*, but as movie-length sketch-comedy efforts go, *Zoolander* is right up there with *Wayne's World* and *Austin Powers*. Speaking of Austin Powers, a shared-universe film with him and Derek Zoolander would be the bomb.

Plus: The menu pages. Gas pump tragedy. Le Tigre. The outfits. Zoolander speaks. Owen Wilson's awesome work as Zoolander's sidekick. Milla Jovovich playing Natasha in an X-rated parody of *Rocky and Bullwinkle*. 2001 gag: "You have 1,200 messages." Ferrari. Gas-pump-water-fountain stinger. Mugatu hair. Blue Steel. The walk-off. The cameos and stunt casting, including David Duchovny as a hand-model conspiracy nutter; Jon Voight as Derek's coal miner father; David Bowie; Fabio; Paris Hilton; Donatella Versace; Natalie Portman; Cuba Gooding, Jr.; Gary Shandling; Winona Ryder; Christian Slater; and Billy Zane.

Minus: Blackface (Why)? A bit vapid at times. Perhaps a bit long. Zoolander is shallow as fuck.

Shelf/Bin: I'm surprised I'm saying this, but this one is a keeper. It was a lot of fun, and my wife also really dug it.

The Hills Run Red (1966)

The box says: "A gripping and powerful tale of retribution, Western style! Revenge is never easy. And in this 'slambang' (*Film Daily*) western full of 'fast-paced action' (*Boxoffice*) and 'mounting suspense' (*Motion Picture Herald*), revenge is never sweeter, either! At the end of the Civil War, Confederate soldier Jerry Brewster (Thomas Hunter) is jailed for a heist engineered by his buddy Ken Seagall (Nando Gazzolo), who escapes with the loot and builds quite a fortune for himself. While suffering behind bars, Brewster realizes he was double-crossed...and vows revenge! Upon his release five years later, Brewster teams up with a stranger named Getz (Dan Duryea) to brawl and shoot his way through Seagall's henchmen and finally settle the score with his old partner-in-crime."

Why I risked a dollar: I made this

rare dollar-movie acquisition at Half Price Books mostly because I was into Westerns at the time, and based on a glance at the film's packaging, I thought it was a classic American Western from the MGM library. When I got it home and looked it up, I realized that I was mistaken and the film is a Spaghetti Western dressed up to look like an American release.

Thoughts: I was a bit disappointed with the film upon discovering it is not an American Western. Don't get me wrong, I have enjoyed my fair share of foreign Westerns over the years, but when I picked this one up, I was hoping to explore the genre's homegrown roots. By the time I got around to watching the film, however, I was past my initial disappointment and found *The Hills Run Red* to be a fairly exciting, if somewhat uninspired, outing.

Plus: A very charismatic and menacing turn from Henry Silva as Mexican henchman Garcia Mendez. Fast-paced. Plenty of punch-ups, shoot-outs, and explosions to keep things moving. Great Ennio Morricone score. Loris Loddi (*Ladyhawke*)'s turn as the brave young son. Thrilling stunt work.

Minus: Choppy editing. A pretty run-of-the-mill revenge story. Lackluster cast.

Shelf/Bin: I think I am going to bin this one. It's not that it's bad, it's just not great either. Besides, this film is now available on Blu-ray with audio commentary, so if I ever hanker to view it again, I'll probably pick up that release.

Scooby-Doo! and KISS: Rock and Roll Mystery (2015)

The box says: "Get ready to Rock! Scooby-Doo and the Mystery Inc. Gang team up with the one and only KISS in this all-new, out-of-this-world adventure! We join the Gang at KISS World, the all-things-KISS theme park, as they investigate a series of strange hauntings. With help from Kiss, they discover that the Crimson Witch has returned to summon The Destroyer from the alternate dimension of KISSteria! The evil duo's ghastly plan to destroy the earth! Can the Gang's cunning and Kiss's power of rock save the day?! Tune in to this Rock and Roll Mystery for some thunderous, heavy FUN!"

Why I risked a dollar: This was one of those films I already liked when I found it for cheap, so I snatched it up not so much to review, but to keep for my collection. How could I pass up a brand-new copy of a film that I wanted to own, and for a mere dollar

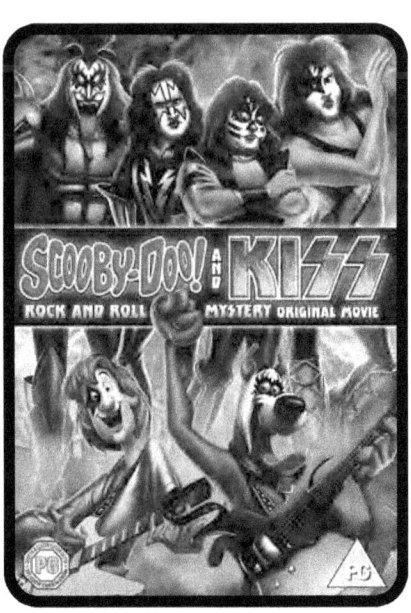

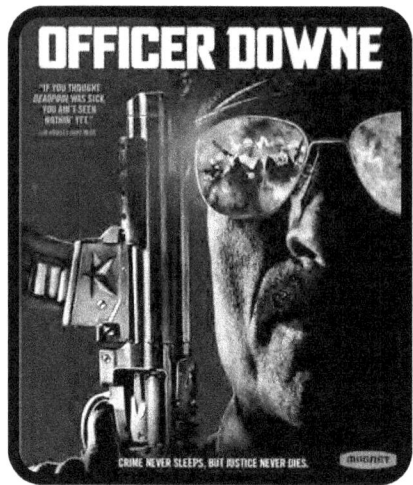

at that?

Thoughts: As a lifelong *Scooby-Doo* fan, I can't tell you when I first saw the show, only that I have watched it for as long as I remember watching TV. As one of the more current direct-to-video *Scooby-Doo* offerings, this film is good entertainment. While not as good as the benchmark *Scooby-Doo on Zombie Island*, it's a good deal better than many of the other entries in the franchise I have seen lately.

Plus: Well-animated. A bunch of great KISS songs. A host of KISS history and Easter eggs. A twitchy Fred (This mystery may be more than his sanity can take). A Jay and Silent Bob cameo. Great voice cast, including the then-current lineup of KISS, Matthew Lillard as "Shaggy," Frank Welker as "Scooby-Doo" and "Fred Jones" (Welker has voiced "Fred" since 1969), Jennifer Carpenter as "Chikara," Penny Marshall as "The Elder," and Hootie and the Blowfish's Darius Rucker as "The Destroyer." The Scooby gang in KISS makeup: priceless.

Minus: A bit too much acid-tripping for its own good. Not much of a mystery to be solved.

Shelf/Bin: This one is a keeper. As I said, I'm a lifelong fan of the show. In fact, I'd rented this film not long ago, so I was pretty excited to add it to my shelves.

Officer Downe (2016)

The box says: "Take a ride along in a hyper-real Los Angeles for the story of a savage L.A. policeman who is repeatedly resurrected and returned to active duty through dark science technology. When a rookie officer is recruited as backup, he discovers there's much more to the reputed super-cop than a mindless law enforcement drone warring against a twisted rogue gallery of over-the-top super-villains. From the graphic novel by Joe Casey and Chris Burnham."

Why I risked a dollar: An eye-catching, foil-embossed slipcover and some nuns with guns on the back cover made the film seem like a winner.

Thoughts: I had high hopes for this when I tossed its shiny box into my basket. Not only was I not let down, I was very pleased with how much fun it was. *Officer Downe* is a fantastic, over-the-top B movie that was adapted from a graphic novel and makes full use of its R rating. I was also impressed with Kim Coates (*The Last Boy Scout*), who somehow delivers a performance that is so much more than just the Robocop/Judge Dredd clone I expected.

Plus: Orgasm counter! Goofy-fun monster boardrooms, gun-dealing nuns, and badly dubbed kung fu masters! Great effects. A good deal of the ultra-violence. Two of the best head-blasts since *Scanners*. Great *Baretta* quote. End credits cartoon.

Minus: An ultra-violent vigilante-cop antihero might not be an easy sell in today's climate. In fact, many things in this outing may offend someone. The side characters are mostly forgettable. The film is kind of derivative and cartoonish.

Shelf/Bin: This one has more than earned its place on my shelf, and I can't wait to watch it again with some friends.

Bait (2012)

The box says: "When a monstrous freak tsunami hits a sleepy beach community, a group of survivors from different walks of life find themselves trapped inside a submerged grocery store. As they try to escape to safety, they soon discover that there is a predator among them more deadly than the threat of drowning—vicious great white sharks lurking in the water, starved for fresh meat. As the bloodthirsty sharks begin to pick the survivors off one by one, the group realizes that they must work together to find a way out without being eaten alive."

Why I risked a dollar: I was actively looking for this film, as I had seen the trailer and thought it looked like fantastic fun. When I found it on the shelves for a dollar, I snatched it up with glee.

Thoughts: I remember, decades ago, reading something on *Ain't It Cool News* (or some other now-defunct movie-rumors website) about a proposed sequel to *Deep Blue Sea* in which a tidal wave knocks a high-rise hotel into the ocean, turning it into a sort of *Poseidon Adventure* with super smart sharks swimming about and eating hotel guests. The *Bait* trailer reminded me of this epic idea, albeit on a much smaller scale and budget. As I watched the film, I realized it was much more sharks-in-a-convenience-store than the *Poseidon Adventure*-like scenario I was hoping for, but it was still a really fun, top-notch thrill ride

Plus: Believable, mostly likable characters. Great sets. A stand-out performance from Julian McMahon (*Nip/Tuck*). Mexican standoff meets wall of water. Body floating away from its arm. Animatronic sharks! Spiders! Leaping sharks! Buckets of gore.

Minus: Not all the special effects succeed. Some of the comedy falls flat.

Shelf/Bin: This one is a keeper and up on the shelf already.

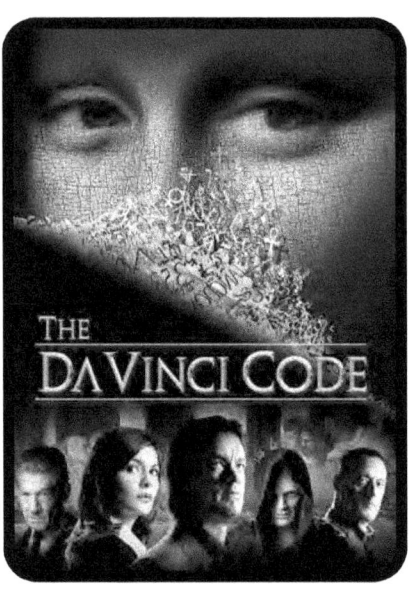

The Da Vinci Code (2006)

The box says: "Dan Brown's international bestseller comes alive in the film The Da Vinci Code, directed by Ron Howard with a screenplay by Akiva Goldsman. Join symbologist Robert Langdon (Academy Award® winner Tom Hanks, 1993 Best Actor, Philadelphia, and 1994 Best Actor, Forrest Gump) and cryptologist Sophie Neveu (Audrey Tautou) in their heart-racing quest to solve a bizarre murder mystery that will take them from France to England—and behind the veil of a mysterious ancient society, where they discover a secret protected since the time of Christ. With first-rate performances by Sir Ian McKellen, Alfred Molina and Jean Reno, critics are calling The Da Vinci Code 'involving' and 'intriguing,' 'a first rate thriller.'"

Why I risked a dollar: Like nearly everyone else in the early 2000s, I read Dan Brown's juggernaut bestseller The Da Vinci Code. I enjoyed it quite a bit and read the first novel soon after. Turns out that Angels and Demons is almost exactly the same book, and I forgot about both of them soon after. Even though the Da Vinci Code movie came out only a few years after I read the book, I didn't really have an urge to check it out. Almost two decades later, I saw it on the dollar shelf at my local Exchange and thought it was time to give the film a shot.

Thoughts: As I said, I remember really liking the novel and thinking it was pretty fast-paced. The film, on the other hand, seems listless and somewhat trivial. Also, while I admit it's been a long time since I read the book, I find it hard to believe that the hero, Robert Langdon, is as pathetic as he is portrayed by the lackluster Tom Hanks.

Plus: Great supporting cast, including Ian McKellen, Alfred Molina, Jürgen Prochnow, Jean Reno, and Paul Bettany. McKellen saying, "You may pass." Nice location choices.

Minus: It's a very unengaging film that takes forever to get started and just seems to jump from encounter to encounter. Ideas that seemed vaguely possible in the novel seem utterly preposterous in the film. The dialogue is clunky, and the climax occurs in the middle of film. The menacing Silas has been mostly neutered. Hanks's heart just does not seem to be in it.

Shelf/Bin: This is going to the bin for sure. I found the movie hard to sit through, and I can't see myself ever trying to do so again.

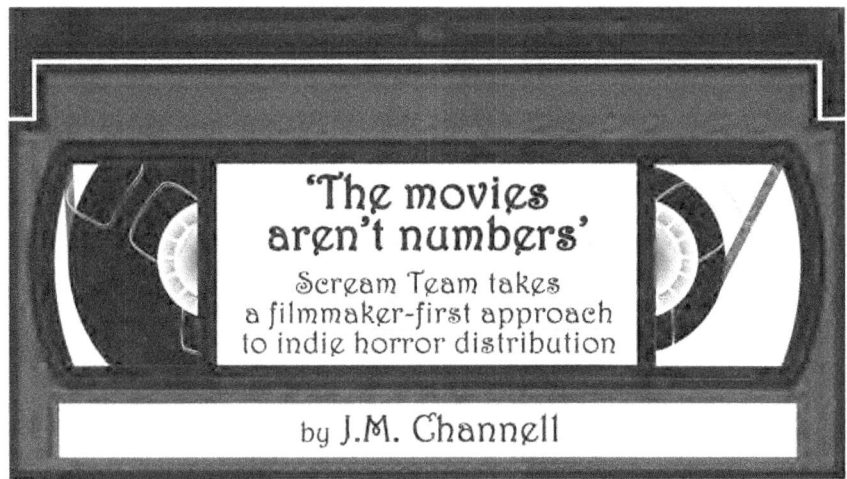

'The movies aren't numbers'

Scream Team takes a filmmaker-first approach to indie horror distribution

by J.M. Channell

When Justin Seaman completed his 2018 film *The Barn*, he faced a new challenge. After spending years conceiving, producing, and promoting the film, he struggled to decide what to do with distribution. Seaman had made a big splash in the indie horror market thanks to relentless promotion at horror conventions and film festivals, as well as a video game, a vinyl soundtrack, and other cross-promotional efforts. However, the waters for distribution—both physical and video on demand—seemed lukewarm at best.

"The goal of *The Barn* was to make back the cost of the feature," Seaman explained, "because I was in such debt. So, I spent a year going around to all of the distribution companies I could."

The search resulted in many nightmare stories from other filmmakers. So, Seaman started to grill some of the distributors about the possibility of making a return on his film. Finally, he found a few who were honest with him.

"[They] said, 'If you're lucky, in five years, you might see $2,000 come back,'" Seaman said. "That very much told me that nobody was going to sell my movie harder than I would, because I was in a situation where I needed to make this money."

As a result, Seaman weighed

his options and decided that self-distributing *The Barn* was his best chance at seeing a return on his investment. Using the same promotional tactics he learned from the prerelease promotion, Seaman and his producing partner, Zane Hershberger, set about handling distribution on their own under their production company moniker, Nevermore Productions. Their efforts paid off, with *The Barn* getting a much-coveted sale order from Family Video—the once-last-remaining-and-since-closed video rental store chain—and deals from various video-on-demand platforms.

After the success of *The Barn*, independent filmmakers began to approach Seaman about distributing their films in the same fashion. While he was flattered by their enthusiasm, Seaman had no interest in becoming a distributor. After all, indie horror film distributors were the same types of companies he was discouraged from joining with his own film. Why would he want to be on the other side of the equation?

"I said, 'Absolutely not.' I'm not a distributor. They have a very bad rep that comes along with that."

However, when Seaman and Hershberger produced segments for the Halloween-themed anthology film *10/31* for their *Barn* musical collaborator Rocky Gray, they found themselves with another distribution pitch. Gray was planning a self-distribution route similar to what Seaman and Hershberger had pulled off with *The Barn*, but he realized very quickly that he just didn't have the time or energy to do it himself.

"He hit me up one day and said, 'You're going to all these conventions and doing all this stuff with *The Barn* still. How would you feel if I gave you a cut of sales and you took *10/31* along with you?'"

Seaman was still hesitant to take on the endeavor, but Gray noted that he and Hershberger were also involved as directors on *10/31*, and it wouldn't be that much of a stretch to sell it alongside *The Barn*.

"I looked at it like, he's right," Seaman said. "So, I started taking *10/31* to shows, and it sold really well. It sold equally as well as *The Barn* was selling at that time, because I was hitting up a lot of shows where people already had [*The Barn*]. So, I had something to be like, 'Hey, I have something new.'"

The increased exposure led to even more indie filmmakers approaching Seaman with an interest in him distributing their films, and since things were working out well with *10/31*, Seaman began to reconsider his stance on entering the realm of distributing for other filmmakers, but with one important difference from other distributors: "Do it for the filmmakers—do it the right way."

Because releasing other filmmakers' projects under the Nevermore Productions moniker wouldn't make sense, the venture was given a new name: Scream Team Releasing. But the name is not just a clever rhyme: The films the company acquires often provide a valuable opportunity for cross-promotion.

"I was very open with the filmmakers where I would tell them one-on-one, 'I don't know what you spent on your film, and I'd love to help you, but I'm going to be completely

The pumpkin-headed killer from *The Barn* (Photo courtesy and copyright Justin Seaman.)

honest with you: I'll never be able to put the kind of passion and hustle and everything into your film to sell it to make the kind of money for you that I made for myself than you can. Now, I will completely take your movies to conventions and sell them and everything, but what made my movie so sellable was that I went out there and I sold myself. I sold my story, and that's what people want. They want to meet the person that made that movie and hear their story. And they want to buy that movie and that story from you directly.'"

The titular team continues to grow from its humble beginnings, gradually adding critically acclaimed horror films to a diverse roster of horror titles that includes *I'm Dreaming of a White Doomsday*, a bleak postapocalyptic Christmas thriller from Pennsylvania-based effects artist-turned-director Mike Lombardo; Shawn Jones's *Camp Killer*, the Baltimore-lensed "slasher version of *My Dinner with Andre*"; and Jason Zink's punk subculture thriller, *Straight Edge Kegger*.

With horror conventions spread across the United States, Seaman and Hershberger can't possibly cover all the necessary ground in person. Scream Team's strategy is to instead offer filmmakers the chance to represent the company at cons held on their respective turfs. While this may sound like putting a filmmaker to work for their distributor, Seaman notes that this is a vital point of what he's found works in marketing a film.

"When people are buying your film at a con, they're essentially buying your story," Seaman explained. "The cool thing about being able to start a distribution company and continue doing it—because it's been my full-time job for four years now—is that I get to meet so many cool filmmakers, and they work with me. I send them out to shows, and they represent the

"Trick or...AAAAH!" (*The Barn* photo courtesy and copyright Justin Seaman.)

team, and they become friends. I've actually brought those filmmakers out to the sets of my films, so it's cool. It's like a family."

There's also an added benefit for filmmakers who sign up for the full Scream Team promotional experience at conventions: "Whatever film they made and are promoting is usually the biggest seller that weekend," Seaman said, attributing the push in sales to his philosophy that convention attendees are more likely to purchase a film if they've made a personal connection with the filmmaker.

But this is not to say that Seaman only expects himself and other filmmakers to promote their own work. He notes that some of his favorite moments are getting the chance to recommend the films he's distributing, especially when he knows a film will fit in perfect with a convention attendee's particular interests, and especially when he's connecting with budding future filmmakers.

"When kids in high school come up to the table, I'll recommend movies that are a bit rougher and tell them to watch it," he explained. "But then, I tell them to watch the second movie on the disc and see how much [the directors] have grown as filmmakers."

Scream Team's limited-release and filmmaker-focused strategy gives the company a unique advantage in a crowded market of content, an advantage that's especially beneficial in a time when store shelves rarely stock independent films and have their own set of caveats at that level.

"The majority of online sales are from the [Scream Team] website and Amazon; I try to stray away from the Walmart sales," Seaman said, noting that Scream Team does work with a sub-distributor for other online retailers, but not the full brick-and-mortar retail experience. "Getting into the stores, that's where you get yourself into trouble, because of the orders. They want you to manufacture so many units, and if those units don't sell, they ship them back to you. From my standpoint, I'm a smaller business. I eliminate that risk. But I have to keep it elsewhere because not everybody comes to these shows, and not everybody trusts a website they don't know, so you gotta put things on Amazon."

Unfortunately, those buying through Amazon will pay a bit more for shipment from their favorite retailer. As Seaman explains, the additional fees charged to sell on Amazon make it necessary to charge a slightly higher price. This kind of issue is why Seaman feels fine with sticking to e-commerce instead of retailers.

"Distribution is shady. Even trying to be a good person, the network of getting further in to make the

connections…there's just snakes everywhere," he said. "Getting connections for retail, you just can't trust anyone. Even navigating for my own people, it's like, 'How come we can't get to this?' and 'How come we can't get to that?' And I don't want to throw people under the bus, but there are companies that facilitate certain things, and you just can't trust them. And I'm not doing it. I'm not putting these people in this situation where a year from now, when I've not received anything back, [the filmmaker] is going to question me. As much as it would be cool to see your movie in a Walmart, on the shelf, would you rather see that and never see money or just see it on dot-com and make a bit of money? That's the trade-off."

While Blu-ray and DVD purchases make up the bulk of Scream Team's sales, the company has also seen success on various VOD services. Though profit margins are narrow on these services, changing viewer habits make them necessary for finding an audience. Scream Team titles can be found on such streaming services as Tubi, Plex, and Peacock. Notably, *Straight Edge Kegger* spread to a wider audience via word-of-mouth after it was licensed for AMC's Shudder app. However, the rising demand for streaming has caused minor dips in sales.

"Up until the pandemic, I stayed strictly physical," Seaman said. "The pandemic has changed a lot. People have started to just want to stream everything. So, in the past two years, I've started to go digital with a few titles because that's what people want. It's affected physical somewhat, but I'm also selling to collectors. These people want the covers, reversible artwork, and bells and whistles and stuff."

Because the ad-supported and subscription models of VOD streaming may cut down on the blind buys, Seaman notes the method of making personal connections with horror fans is all the more important. Piracy can also be an issue, as is noted clearly in Scream Team's pre-menu warning screens, which ask the viewer to please not torrent the disc. However, thanks to the company's focus on filmmaker support and forming personal connections with customers, piracy seems to be a minor problem for the Scream Team family.

"The heart of it is conventions where you meet people who want physical media. They crave it. That's why I do so many of these shows."

However, making these kinds of personal connections with fans and filmmakers does require keeping Scream Team at a manageable scale. As a result, the label only releases about four to six titles per year to keep the operation from growing too big and to avoid mission drift from Seaman's goal of creating a label that's for filmmakers. The reasoning is grounded in the central idea behind the label's success.

"The movies aren't numbers. I'm picking up the person and their story."

Check out Scream Team Releasing at: https://screamteamreleasing.com/.

FORCE OF ZANE HERSHBERGER

I met The Barn's DP, Zane Hershberger, "back in the day" when we both worked in the converted slaughterhouse that was the WRS Motion Picture and Video Lab. (You know the story about Night of the Living Dead producer Russ Streiner playing chess with a lab owner for NOTLD's developing fees and winning because the owner couldn't play chess to save his life? It's that lab.) Working there, we knew we were bound for greater things, because, quite frankly, it couldn't have gotten any worse. What's fun now is seeing him at conventions rather than in the dark, uglily tiled halls of the lab.

"My journey between WRS and starting with The Barn was filled with several false starts," Zane told me. "First, it was on a project called The Hideout; and then a couple faux trailers; a feature we filmed that will never see the light of day, The Residual; a short film we won an award for called Devilution; and then working as a jack-of-all-trades on a feature called Captain Happy Sun. Once I got involved with The Barn, things fell into place, and my confidence as a DP and a filmmaker in general grew exponentially."

As most savvy horror fans know, Justin Seaman's The Barn was "the little indie horror movie that could." After Amazon's shocking indie purge half a dozen years back, The Barn's appearance on the scene was proof that there was still a market for indie

Hershberger (left) directing *Force to Fear* (Image courtesy and copyright Zane Hershberger.)

horror, although the pathways were narrower and more treacherous than ever. Much of *The Barn*'s success, however, hinged on its crucial look: the loving emulation of '80s slashers. And that look was thanks to Zane Hershberger.

"I started on *The Barn* as a 2nd unit cameraman," said Zane. "Then, after the movie was shot and Justin wasn't happy with the original DP's results, he asked me to come in and reshoot the majority of the movie to make it more in line with the vision he wanted."

This was a good move on Seaman's part. It led to additional collaborations on *10/31*, *Cryptids*, "several other short films," and most recently, *Force to Fear*.

Like the best indie movies, *Force to Fear* isn't just one thing or the other. It splashes around in the same pool as '80s wacko movies produced by Cannon and De Laurentiis. It begins as one type of film and then becomes something else. Summarized: *"Two kidnappers, a dealer, a group of college kids, and a killer converge in an abandoned school. Once they cross paths, chaos ensues, and it's a race to survive the night."*[1]

"*Force to Fear* came from my friend and cocreator, Chad Bruns," said Zane. "He approached me with a concept for a feature that he and I both expanded on when he found out we had access to an entire school as a location in Weirton, West Virginia. So, we knew a couple actors we wanted to work with and designed characters specifically for them and began to plan out all the fight choreography for the movie. We also reached out to the talented musician Matt Cannon to make us a score that complements the '80s action/thriller aesthetic we were looking for."

The Barn, *10/31*, and *Force to Fear* are all available streaming and through Screamteamreleasing.com.

---

1 "Storyline." *IMDb*, IMDb.com, Inc., https://www.imdb.com/title/tt10176540/.

**Back issue pages like REAL magazines used to have!
I mean, ALSO FROM HAPPY CLOUD MEDIA, LLC:**

Exploitation Nation—Premiere Issue! We kick off with everyone's favorite sub-genre: the **Lesbian Vampire Film**. In this premiere issue, Dyanne Thorne interview; "lost" interviews with Clive Barker and his *Saint Sinner* stars, Mary Mara, Rebecca Harrell. Plus reviews! $5.99

#2: Cryptids of the Cinema: Bigfoot, Nessie, The Mothman, The Yeti, The Pope Lick Monster - we got 'em all! Well, most. The monsters and the movies that love them. Also this issue, journalist Mike Watt takes a look back at his time covering 2009's *Sorority Row*. Plus, bidding a fond farewell to **George A. Romero**. $7.99

#3: Bizarro Films. Contributions from Heather Drain and John Skipp. PLUS: Jose Mojica Marins, aka "Coffin Joe"; an interviews with filmmakers Rolfe Kanefsky; Greg DeLiso and Peter Litvin, and EXCLUSIVE INTERVIEW with Stephen Sayadian (aka "Rinse Dream"). $7.99

#4: Rock 'n Roll Movies! 144-pages! Interviews with Paul Bunnell (*The Ghastly Love of Johnny X*); Jon-Mikl Thor and Frank Dietz (*Rock 'n Roll Nightmare*); *Slade in Flame*; AIP's *Beach Party* films; Prince on Film; goodbye to Harlan Ellison; Richard Elfman on *Forbidden Zone*. $7.99

#5: Alternate Reality Warning: not a single title in this book is real. Interviewee Larry Blamire ("The Lost Skeleton Cadavra") is real, but the interview isn't. Plus: The Beatles' adapt *Lord of the Rings*, directed by Stanley Kubrick; David Lynch directs *Revenge of the Jedi*; Amos Poe's remake of *Alphaville* with Debbie Harry; the film adaptation *A Field Guide to Film Gods*. ALL HAIL CINEMAGOG! $7.99

#6: Underground Comix! Did your old man throw YOURS away? Interviews with: Stephen Bissette, Trina Robbins, Mike Diana, Frank Henenlotter, Greg Ketter, Mark Bode, Howard Cruse's final interview; plus Buddy Giovinazzo, Vaughn Bode's final essay, *Confessions Of A Cartoon Gooroo*.

Note: #6 Boasts two covers, sold separately: $7.99 each

**Back issue pages like REAL magazines used to have!
I mean, ALSO FROM HAPPY CLOUD MEDIA, LLC:**

#7: Indie Filmmaking issue! * Mark Savage and his new film *Purgatory Road*; James L. Edwards and *Her Name Was Christa** Gabe Bartalos and his newest, *Saint Bernard** Scooter McCrae and his adventures with the British censorship; Carmine Capobianco (*Psychos in Love*); Henrique Couto (*Babysitter Massacre*); Revjen Miller (*The Adventures of Electra Elf*). $7.99

#8: Witnesses for the Defense! Our writers to defend a movie only they seem to like. From *Grease 2* to *Ernest Goes to Jail* to *Godzilla '98*. PLUS an **exclusive interview with director Terry Gilliam** and *The Man Who Killed Don Quixote*! $7.99

#9: When Nature (and Elder Gods) Attack! Cover by interviewee **Tom Sullivan** (*Evil Dead*)! PLUS a tribute to Stuart Gordon; Lovecraft movies; Tippi Hedren tries to kill her family in *Roar!*, Asian Worm Horror! And much more! $7.99

#10: Comedy is HARD! Interviews with **James Lorinz** (*Frankenhooker*), **Jason Paul Collum**, and **Josh Miller/Pat Casey** (writers, *Sonic the Hedgehog* articles by Carmine Capobianco (*Psychos in Love*), Michael Legge (*Sideshow Entertaiment*), and so much more! $7.99

#11: CULTURE: CANCELLED! *"Everything's been cancelled!"* In this issue, we explore what is and what isn't censorship. Interviews with **Jeff Burr** (*Leatherface*), **Linnea Quigley** (*Silent Night, Deadly Night*), **Alex Cox** (*Repo Man*) and **Jill Schoelen** (*The Stepfather*). PLUS an extensive look at the German Cult Classic, **KILLER CONDOM**, featuring rare artwork by **H.R. Giger** and **Jorg Buttgereit**! $7.99

#12: "We're Still Standing!" Interviews with *Something Weird Video's* **Lisa Petrucci**, and filmmakers **Tim Ritter** and **Thomas Edward Seymour**. Then a sound-off from all of those who survived COVID and are still going! Celebrate indie EVERYTHING! $7.99

Back issue pages like REAL magazines used to have! I mean, ALSO FROM HAPPY CLOUD MEDIA, LLC:

Grindhouse Purgatory #15: In this special issue, we say goodbye to our friend, actor, and mentor, Sid Haig. His friends and fans come from all over contribute remembrances of this amazing man and his incredible career. From his early days starring in Jack Hill's exploitation epics, to his resurgence in *Jackie Brown* and *House of 1,000 Corpses*, Sid was a unique performer and a lovely person. $9.99

Movie Outlaw: The Prequel by Mike Watt is a revamped republishing of what was previously-known as *Fervid Filmmaking*. Featuring essays on 70 underseen films including *Keep Off My Grass*, *Dr. Caligari*, *Forbidden Zone*, *Coonskin*, *Head*, *Psychos in Love*, and many more. A rare interview with director Stephen Sayadian. 350 pages. $15.99

Movie Outlaw by Mike Watt. Essays focusing on more than 70 underseen films including Johnny Depp's directorial debut, *The Brave*; *Don's Plum*; Mauritzio Nichetti's *Volere Volare*; *The Ghastly Love of Johnny X*, the last 35mm black 'n white science fictional musical ever made! 472 pages. $19.99

Movie Outlaw Rides Again! By Mike Watt. Essays on 70 underseen films: *Crazy Moon*; *Frankenhooker*; *Jane White is Sick and Twisted*; *The Magic Christian*, *Meet the Feebles*; *Impure Thoughts*; *The Stunt Man*; *Night Breed*; Brian DePalma's *Phantom of the Paradise*, Will Vinton's *The Adventures of Mark Twain*; *The Redsin Tower*. 392 pages. $19.99

Son of the Return of Movie Outlaw by Mike Watt. Essays include: *Accion Mutante*; Ralph Bakshi's *Heavy Traffic*; *Down and Dirty Duck*; *The Thief and the Cobbler*; *The Sinful Dwarf*; *Performance*; *Muppets Most Wanted*; *Legend of Simon Conjurer*; *Sorority Babes in the Slimeball Bowl-O-Rama*; *Shock Treatment*; *Yellowbeard*. Interviews with Jon Voight and Ralph Bakshi! 352 pages. $19.99

Hot Splices by Mike Watt. Eight interwoven tales about the Film Addicts, the Cinephages who devour film for the high, the bleeding perforations in their skin is just part of the game. There are five forbidden films that can induce madness or release the Dark Gods that created them, speaking through the psychopathic director. Fiction. $14.99

Order today at www.happycloudpublishing.com!

LIKE WHAT YOU SEE?
LOVE EXPLOITATION NATION?

TELL THE WORLD!

Independent art lives and dies by word-of-mouth. If you dig Exploitation Nation, collected all the issues, bought the t-shirt, the chewing gum, and our lead-free housepaint, please share the love!

Link to our Facebook Page:
https://www.facebook.com/ExploitationNation

And, as always, visit:
www.happycloudpictures.net

SEE YOU NEXT ISSUE!

www.ingramcontent.com/pod-product-compliance
Lightning Source LLC
Chambersburg PA
CBHW071321040426
42444CB00009B/2064